Irish Cases in Entrepreneurship

Edited By

THOMAS M. COONEY

BLACKHALL
PUBLISHING

This book was typeset by Ashfield Press for

BLACKHALL PUBLISHING
33 Carysfort Avenue
Blackrock
Co. Dublin
Ireland

e-mail: info@blackhallpublishing.com
www.blackhallpublishing.com

© Individual contributors, 2005

ISBN: 1 842180 87 8

A catalogue record for this book is available from the British Library.

Printed in Ireland by
ColourBooks Ltd

Foreword

Entrepreneurship contributes to job creation and economic growth and is crucial to innovation and competitiveness. From a wider societal perspective, it provides many benefits including greater potential for work satisfaction and wider consumer choice. Clearly, Ireland's ability to grow ambitious, globally competitive enterprises will be a key determinant of its future success. Enterprise Ireland is strongly committed to encouraging the growth of entrepreneurial start-ups. Since 1999, it has assisted the establishment of almost 270 high potential companies. These enterprises are typically innovation-driven and knowledge-based and are characterised by ambitious export, sales and development targets. They stem from a variety of promising sectors including biotechnology, photonics, IT, medical devices and functional foods, and from a number of backgrounds. Some are the direct result of research in our third level institutions that have led to the formation of campus companies. Others are the creation of serial entrepreneurs who have realised value from their previous businesses and are prepared to re-invest in a new venture, and still more are emerging from people who have the courage to leave the relative comfort of secure employment to realise their own business venture. While emerging from different sources, entrepreneurs all share one vital attribute – the drive and ambition to grow their own businesses.

The 2003 Global Entrepreneurship Monitor (GEM) Report found that Ireland is one of the most entrepreneurially active countries in Europe. Ireland needs to maintain this position of prominence and to further embed a supportive entrepreneurial environment in which even greater numbers of these innovative new companies can be created and developed to a position of strength in global markets. It therefore behoves us, as policymakers and as citizens, to support them and to encourage them in every way possible. The Irish Academy of Management plays an important role in this through its promotion of research and education on organisation and management issues. Enterprise Ireland is pleased to work with the Academy on this book, *Irish Cases in Entrepreneurship*, which draws together a number of case studies on the wide range of issues inherent in entrepreneurship. Their valuable insights warrant reflection by all those wishing to participate in or to support future entrepreneurial activity in Ireland.

DR MARTIN LYES

Science & Innovation
Enterprise Ireland

ENTERPRISE
IRELAND

ENTERPRISE IRELAND is the Irish government agency responsible for the development of Irish industry. It works in partnership with more than 3,000 client companies to help them build their competitive advantage in the global marketplace.

Its clients primarily comprise of:
- Manufacturing and internationally traded services companies employing ten or more people
- Entrepreneurs with the ability to initiate projects that can compete in international markets
- Irish-based food and natural resource companies that are overseas-owned or controlled.

Through its 13 Irish and 33 international offices, it provides advisory and financial support to those wishing to:
- Start a business
- Grow their business
- Enter new export markets
- Use R&D and innovative practices to improve productivity and competitiveness
- Source new world-class suppliers from Ireland.

In 2003, Enterprise Ireland clients achieved overseas sales of €10.2 billion (total sales including domestic turnover amounted to €25.1 billion) and employed 142,045 staff; 61 new high potential start-up companies were supported by the agency in the same period.

www.enterprise-ireland.com

Irish Academy of Management

THE IRISH ACADEMY OF MANAGEMENT is the leading professional association for management research and education on the island of Ireland. The purpose of the Irish Academy of Management is to promote the advancement of research, knowledge and education in the field of organisation and management studies.

To further its purpose, the Academy pursues the following objectives:

- To build wider appreciation and acceptance of the science and practice of management
- To provide opportunities for researchers to collaborate within and across the sub-area specialities of management
- To encourage presentation and publication of scholarly research.

The *Irish Journal of Management* is the official journal of the Irish Academy of Management. The Journal Incorporates IBAR (Irish Business and Administrative Research). The Journal aims to contribute to a wider understanding of the nature, characteristics and performance for both Irish and international organisations through the dissemination of research from a wide variety of management-related areas. Papers are welcomed from both traditional management disciplines and from the new and emerging interdisciplinary areas.

www.iamireland.com

Ireland's Network of Teachers and Researchers of Entrepreneurship (INTRE)

INTRE has been established to provide a network for those working within the area of entrepreneurship in third level institutions on the island of Ireland. The Board of INTRE is constituted by one representative from each institution who champions the work of INTRE and the field of entrepreneurship within their own institution. The following are the objectives of INTRE as agreed at the first Board meeting:

- To create a greater understanding of the broader definition of entrepreneurship
- To develop the interface between business and technology within each institution
- To increase the receptivity of stakeholders in the provision of entrepreneurship teaching in training programmes across faculties
- To map out the work currently being done in Irish institutions
- To raise the level of activity in entrepreneurship education
- To raise the media profile of Irish academics in this area
- To generate increased research funding
- To encourage and promote collaborative work
- To achieve widespread recognition of INTRE as the principal Irish network for teachers and researchers of entrepreneurship
- To develop an active network of teachers and researchers working in the area of entrepreneurship education
- To increase the number of posts and chairs in entrepreneurship
- To increase the output of publications on entrepreneurship

- To give the Irish academic community substantial representation and recognition in the international entrepreneurship arena.

For further information on joining INTRE, please contact your local representative or Dr Thomas Cooney at thomas.cooney@dit.ie.

Contents

CASE
STUDIES

I

Altobridge[1]

BREDA O'DWYER and ANN SEARS[2]

As Mike Fitzgerald, CEO of Altobridge, was leaving the office on Friday evening, he had a lot to think about for the week ahead. There was an important meeting overseas with a potential strategic partner where Mike needed to find funding and customers for the continued development of his company. He was proud that Altobridge was at the centre of developments in delivering personal mobile telephony to the maritime and civil aviation markets. However, there were barriers for this type of product in the aviation industry due to the possible interference involved with communicating via a mobile phone while air travelling due to an airplane's technology. While Altobridge was at the test stage for some of their products, they knew that once the products entered the commercialisation stage they could then target different niche markets.

THE COMPANY

Mike Fitzgerald has the classic traits of an Irish entrepreneur. He is from a family that runs its own business, he received his undergraduate degree in Computer Science and Mathematics and is pursuing a Masters Degree in Commerce. Mike was previously Vice President of two NASDAQ quoted companies and he led an MBO of Microcellular Systems from ADC Telecommunications and went on to complete a successful trade sale of that company for $20 million in 2001. He gained multiple senior level international experiences while working for Ericsson. Fitzgerald is a board member of several Irish technology companies including Propylon Limited (XML solutions for mobile communication) and Red Circle (Voice Portal Solutions). Altobridge was established in 2002 after Mike noticed a gap in the market for developing a product that would allow global communications anytime, anywhere.

Since the founding of Altobridge, key players who have particular experience and expertise have been placed within the company and on the Board of the company. Currently Altobridge has five Board members who come from a variety of backgrounds, including areas such as accountancy, law, telecommunications and electronic engineering. The management team constitutes the director of business development, director of R&D, the head of product development and the director of regulatory affairs. The Altobridge management team has an impressive proven track record in the development and launch of leading-edge wireless solutions such as transportable emergency wireless networks on wheels and the world's first mass market wireless service on cruise ships. Additionally, Altobridge's management team experienced first hand the dramatic drive for Micro Cellular and Pico Cellular technology throughout the period of 1995 to 2002. During this time the team played a leading roll in identifying, designing and successfully deploying new innovative and differentiating value-added wireless applications across the globe, including: In-Building Coverage Solutions, Wireless Office Solutions, Rural Wireless Solutions, Emergency Network Solutions, Underground Solutions and Wireless On Board Ships. It is interesting to note that all members of the management team come from a technological background with one member having worked in the Aeronautical, Land and Maritime industries.

The company currently has over twenty employees and staff turnover is relatively low. It appears that Altobridge has an innovative and flexible working environment where the employees are considered a high valued resource. As a family man, Fitzgerald understands the importance of the work/life balance and incorporates this thinking into the organisational culture.

THE PRODUCTS

One of the most significant challenges that Altobridge presently faces is that it cannot bring some of its products to market because of restrictions set by the aeronautical industry and by the regulators who set the RF (Radio Frequency) levels. These restrictions include the banning of in-flight communications due to the possibility of interference with the airplane's systems. But the regulations regarding the level of RF that are allowable on aircrafts should not be a problem with the product developed by Altobridge because Altobridge eliminates the possibility of interference by dictating very low power levels. 'Certainly, operating at maximum power outputs of 2W, handsets could present an interference problem. However, because our solution is based on GSM technology, we are able to set the power at a much lower and safe level,' says Mike Fitzgerald, CEO of Altobridge. He believes that it remains imperative in this era of continuing acceleration in the use of personal wireless devices, that industry and regulators work together to address the goal of developing devices and systems which will generate no adverse effect on avionics equipment.

While Altobridge has developed a number of options for potential customers on how to deliver in-flight communications to passengers, other barriers face Altobridge's technology, including safety concerns regarding personal in-flight wireless and telephony via individual handsets. Additional R&D at the company is focusing on the patent pending stand-alone fully redundant solution for the aircraft industry that can introduce cellular communications via the IFE system without the need to transmit or receive wirelessly. 'At a time when airlines need a shot in the arm to boost revenues, the Altobridge SIM solution can deliver a much-needed revenue stream through the provision of a personal communications and m-commerce service,' explained Fitzgerald. 'The utilisation of SIM-card technology to bring standard communications devices into the mobile telephony world is not new, but what is unique about the Altobridge architecture is the ability to do so within the bandwidth restrictive environs of the aircraft.'

Altobridge has developed a number of products for targeting of particular markets. The Altobridge AM Gateway Platform™ supports voice calls and text messaging (SMS) in exactly the same way as a land-based GSM network. Subscribers roam onto the airborne network in the same way that a subscriber roams from one country to another. The network architecture that would enable this technology is currently patent pending by Altobridge. This product can be also used within the maritime market. Post 9/11 it became apparent that container shipment security had to be tightened up because of the potential risk ports presented to terrorist attacks. Although there were many solutions for ship tracking prior to this, there was no solution for container security while onboard ships. Altobridge developed a system that would track containers while in motion and thus eliminated the risk factor. With their proposed solution, if someone were to open a container door and place a bomb in it, the owner, the shipping company and the relevant government would all be notified automatically as to the security breech while the ship was still at sea. Within the maritime market Altobridge will also be targeting superyachts, cruise and ferry passenger boats and crew calling.

Altobridge is continuously investing in R&D. They have plans for future products and have 'road mapped' areas for product development. Currently they are having trials on two of their products with partners. For a company that started in 2002, they are certainly investing substantially in new product development, although they have yet to bring a product to market. They had hoped to be doing the trials towards the end of 2003 but that target date was pushed out to the spring of 2004. They had their first trial for in-flight wireless communications with a company based in the US and while that proved to be successful, they must undertake numerous trials to prove that there is no interference with the product before it can go to market.

Mike Fitzgerald has already proved that he is an effective innovator, as his last company Microcellular Systems sold for $20 million. Mike, along with his team of leading industrialist wireless experts, developed a new product that was too early for the market, so he sold the company to a larger company who waited to bring the product to market until the timing was right. This large multinational company is currently enjoying the fruits of the labour of Mike and his team. Had Mike Fitzgerald and the team held on to the company and taken the risk to bring the product to commercialisation, they may have reaped the benefits as the current owners are now doing with the Mike's creation. Such is the choice that faces an entrepreneur on a regular basis.

There now appears to be a new challenge facing Altobridge, whether to put their energies into R&D or bring a product to market and make some sales. For a relatively small company they have been focusing on product development rather than market development. They need to address this issue and make a decision for their future.

The management of Altobridge did decide to a launch a version of their principal product for a niche maritime market, the Superyacht industry. The Superyacht industry comprises of approximately 7,500 superyachts worldwide and these superyachts are typically private vessels over 100 feet in length. Altobridge has been contacted by approximately twenty of the world's leading companies across the globe with regard to distributing this product but they have yet to produce a finished offering.

THE COMPETITION

There are a number of competitors within these markets, including Boeing and AirCell, that are currently developing similar technologies. However, Fitzgerald remarks that: 'We do not see ourselves as being in competition with companies like AirCell. This is potentially a huge market and we need as many players as possible to bring it to critical mass'. Altobridge would have the competitive advantage over competing products due to the fact that they have a product that is currently undergoing trials and the cost of their product is substantially cheaper than the other alternatives leading to continued operational savings for its customers. The key question at the moment is who will be the first to market, as being the pioneer brings a number of advantages and disadvantages. For Altobridge to reach the market first, it needs additional funds for product investment.

THE TARGET MARKET

Despite significant developments in the global wireless applications industry, two major markets have been ignored: wireless communications at sea and wireless communications on aircraft. Altobridge has identified a unique solution that can overcome the technological and regulatory barriers of entry peculiar to these particular market sectors. The company has provided a solution that monitors and manages the RF. Their products will provide easy-to-install, price insensitive wireless communication for the airline industry and a real time container communication system for the sea sector. Altobridge can provide significant added value to these sectors by minimising supply chain disruptions through a scheduled technological tracking reporting mechanism. Mike Fitzgerald estimates that ships and aircraft represent 'the final frontier of GSM coverage' and says Altobridge is 'early in the GSM solution'. The new technologies that are patent pending could open up a potential market of one billion users globally. Fitzgerald states that 'revenue from the Superyacht market, which is the company's smallest projected business unit, is enough to make Altobridge profitable'. He goes on to claim that 'research has shown that the demand for wireless applications in the aviation industry alone is worth several billion dollars a year in recurring revenue through roaming charges'. Currently management is unsure as to whether or not it should target both markets individually or simultaneously. Fitzgerald himself believes that the latter is the most preferred option. However, some of his team members believe that they should roll out their products separately in the two different markets. In fact, Fitzgerald believes that the company should pass on the responsibility of the 'roll out' to another company by formulating a licence agreement and moving on to the next innovative requirements of the wireless industry. Always prepared to listen to his team members, Fitzgerald has requested proposals on how best to target the identified markets.

MARKETING STRATEGY

Presently Mike Fitzgerald's principal concern is the sales and distribution strategy that needs to be developed by the company. Altobridge needs to decide whether to use a direct or indirect channel of distribution. Experience within the management team would prefer indirect distribution by aligning the company with established partners operating in these industries. However, Fitzgerald is also open to the option of recruiting export sales executives with experience of operating within these sectors. He is apprehensive that such personnel might not fit in with the team at Altobridge but he is willing to consider all options.

Other options for Altobridge include identifying a partner for the aviation and marine sector separately or teaming up with an organisation operating in both sectors. Should Altobridge seek partners with technological superiority or should the company seek partners with an established distribution network? Should this network be based across America, Europe, Asia, Middle East and Africa or should Altobridge seek a separate distribution arrangement within each targeted geographic market? As the system is under trials in the US, Fitzgerald sees the business jet market in the US as the first target market. However, he suggested that there was 'no reason to delay entry into the European markets and that the speed of the roll out would be dictated by the availability of funding and by the regulatory environment'.

The decisions taken on the distribution strategy will have significant implications for the promotional strategies to be used by Altobridge in creating awareness and securing contracts within these sectors. The promotional strategy cannot ignore the effective online opportunities afforded to companies promoting within the B2B wireless communications sectors. Technology developments such as CRM (Customer Relationship Management) and RFID (Radio Frequency Identity) have created openings for companies to establish and/or strengthen relationships with customers in these sectors. Altobridge needs to make decisions on how best to distribute their promotional budget across relevant trade show participation, media publications, advertising, direct marketing and personal selling development. However, the critical question remains, where will they get the money and how much do they need for their marketing strategy?

FUNDING

To date the company has raised significant monies from management, staff, private investors and SFADCO (Shannon Free Airport Development Company). The principal issue facing the company at the moment is the need to raise further funds in order to realise future business opportunities in the aeronautical and maritime communications industries. The options that are available to raise funds for the company include: management, staff, strategic partners, customers, competitors, BES (Business Expansion Scheme), Venture Capital, business angels and bank facilitators. Altobridge is conscious of the different requirements of these investors and they need to deliberate carefully on which would be best for the company to pursue. Mike Fitzgerald and his board of directors are aware of the need to incorporate the concept of ownership and equity in their decisions, as they will need to sell some shareholding if they are to get the funds that they so badly need.

THE FUTURE

Realising that the idea is excellent and that a need exists for the products in the marketplace, Fitzgerald is poignantly aware of his dilemma – the need to get the product to the market and to access the money required to do so.

As he is driving away from the office, Fitzgerald's phone rings and his close friend and business partner reminds him of his upcoming interview with Ernst & Young for the Entrepreneur of the Year competition. The questions now going through his head will undoubtedly be addressed during the interview leaving Fitzgerald with a lot of thinking to do over the weekend. One thought that crosses his mind is that maybe he should sell the business and move on to something new again.

NOTES
1. This case is intended to be used as the basis for class discussion rather than to illustrate either effective or ineffective handling of a management situation.
2. Breda O'Dwyer and Ann Sears are Lecturers in Marketing at the Institute of Technology in Tralee.

2

Clodagh Malone[1]

COLETTE HENRY and KATE JOHNSTON[2]

I always had a dream to branch out on my own. OK, I thought,
five years would give me enough experience, but that was a bit
naïve - it really took ten years before I knew enough and even then,
you never really know enough to start your own business!

CLODAGH MALONE

Clodagh Malone started thinking seriously about owning her own business after she graduated from university. A mathematical scientist from Co. Louth, this aspiring entrepreneur had a clear, strategic development plan from the outset. Realising the critical importance of work experience, the DCU (Dublin City University) graduate started out in 1992 as a computer programmer with a small growing company, FMW (Facilities Management Workshop).

While Clodagh has received tremendous support and encouragement from her family in her entrepreneurial endeavours, it is interesting that there was no apparent entrepreneurial tradition for her to follow. Her father was a teacher, a profession which, according to Clodagh, 'insulated' him from the business world. However, both her maternal grandmother and her paternal great-grandmother ran local corner shops and this seemed to be the family's only entrepreneurial history. Thus, the trigger for Clodagh's entrepreneurial tendencies appears to have been her first employer, Rod, who seems to have sown the entrepreneurial seed. Rod was her boss in FMW, a charismatic, highly enthusiastic sort of guy.

FMW, then a privately owned company, was just a six- or seven-person operation when Clodagh joined; a small start-up with a highly dynamic working environment. For Clodagh, this was the most exciting place in which she had worked. She was a programmer, a job that involved trips to Norway. It was an exciting job where often she 'didn't know what was going to happen from one week to the next'. Clodagh was just six months out of college when she joined FMW and it was great experience for her. The company was about three or four years old at that time and was based in the Development Centre, an incubation facility on the campus of Dundalk Institute of Technology. It was a very open environment with a strong team dynamic. It was clear that Rod and FMW had a major positive influence on Clodagh, providing just the right sort of environment needed to fuel her entrepreneurial aspirations.

For personal reasons, which were later revealed to be of a romantic nature (Clodagh's husband-to-be was working in Dublin at the time), Clodagh eventually left FMW to work in Dublin, where she became a contractor for An Post[3]. This was an entirely different experience to that of her first job. While the overall pace of work seemed to be much slower, with lots of meetings, red tape and bureaucracy, Clodagh's actual job was very progressive. Her work at An Post, which involved GIS database development, was very exciting. Clodagh's initial position had actually been with the consultancy company that worked for An Post. This was a dynamic start-up company developed out of UCD (University College Dublin) which closed down due to An Post's decision to take just two staff members (including Clodagh) from the original consultancy team to work on a project. This would obviously give An Post more control over the project.

After two years, Clodagh switched jobs again and began working for Irish Permanent Finance, where she was in charge of new business technology. All this experience gave her 'a taste' of what it would be like to work for a big business, as well as the public sector and a start-up, thus providing her with a broad spectrum of business experience. The An Post experience in particular confirmed to Clodagh that it was the start-up environment that she preferred, one where she could be responsible for everything, including answering the phone, writing her own letters and organising her own business trips. For Clodagh, the openness of a small working environment meant that everyone knew what was going on, leaving little time for office politics, one of the negative characteristics of large organisations.

Working in the city had its advantages and disadvantages for Clodagh and her husband. On the one hand, it was clear that they really enjoyed it – it suited them at that particular time. On the other hand, it was quite a different story once children start to come along. Following the birth of her first child in 1999, Clodagh resigned from Irish Permanent Finance in search of a more flexible working environment. She wanted to work from home and rear her children at the same time. Her contacts in An Post and Irish Permanent proved invaluable in this regard and helped Clodagh to start working from home on the internet, developing websites and small speculative computer programmes. She wrote a system for GAA clubs – 'GAA Club Manager' – and another speculative package for An Post – an optimiser for their staffing in sorting offices. In short, what Clodagh really wanted was flexibility, to work on the internet and 'write code' and to look after their child at the same time; to not have to endure long commuting times to Dublin for a highly structured, inflexible nine-to-five job.

The working hours were an important factor in Clodagh's decision to quit her job. From a practical perspective, working from home gave her total flexibility, sending e-mails when it suited her and not necessarily between the hours of nine and five. Timescales became flexible, allowing her to continue working on a project in order to meet a deadline. She could be at home with her family, which is often easier than trying to organise a babysitter.

In early 2003, both Clodagh and her husband decided to return to live in Dundalk. With two young children, it was clear that returning to their native home town, where their family and friends were based, would provide a better environment for bringing up children. Clodagh's parents lived in Dundalk, as she put it 'just a few fields away', and her husband's lived six miles away.

DEVELOPING THE BUSINESS IDEA

The inspiration for Clodagh's proposed new business came from her work experience and the encouragement of one of her former work colleagues who showed an interest in her idea for a new website. Clodagh was planning to develop a website where people could look up any address in Ireland. The website would not include names as such; rather it would correct or fill in the missing pieces of a postal address. The plan was to get the host website off the ground as a 'shop window' and then possibly move on to deal with the task of correcting addresses.

The postal communications industry in Ireland is receiving increased attention due, in part, to technology changes in the communications systems overall and the drive towards harmonisation as the EU (European Union) continues to expand. For example, although the majority of countries in the EU have a postcoding system, Ireland (like Greece) does not. Dublin and Cork are the only cities in Ireland to have two-digit codes added after postal addresses. Postal communications in Ireland get delayed all the time, particularly at peak times such as Christmas, Easter and New Year, when incorrect or miss-spelt addresses cause letters and parcels to go astray. According to Clodagh's research, only 75 per cent of post gets delivered the next day and around 2 per cent of post has an incorrect address. In general terms, effective deliveries rely on the postman's local knowledge. As the postcode system has worked so effectively in the UK and further afield, it would seem inevitable that Ireland will introduce this or a similar system at some point in the future.

An Post, however, are not convinced that postcoding is necessary in Ireland. They have already invested €110 million since 2000 as part of their current automation programme, with auto-sorting allocated to four centres – Athlone, Cork, Dublin and Portlaoise. They believe that a postcoding/address-correcting system would provide an insufficient basis upon which to build a modern automation programme and see difficulties with implementing such a system as including: high costs, resistance to change and the continued need for all address lines to be read accurately to gain maximum automation benefits. However, there would appear to be a need for further technological development in geolocation applications.

Another key player in the communications industry and a key consideration for Clodagh's new business is ComReg. ComReg is the Commission for Communications Regulation in Ireland and is the statutory body responsible for the regulation of telecommunications, radio communications and broadcasting transmissions. Their remit covers all types of transmission networks, including telephone wires, television and radio, cable, licensing frameworks for satellite services and postal delivery networks. ComReg enables competition in the communications sector by facilitating authorisation to provide networks and services.[4]

In 2002, and with the timing apparently right, Clodagh's husband took voluntary redundancy from his company to join her in her entrepreneurial endeavours. He had a business idea of his own, also in the ICT sector, that he wanted to explore. This product had been 'glaring him in the face' and now, moving back to Dundalk where family support would be better, seemed just the right time for both of them to explore their ideas. The fact that both of them now had the freedom to explore their business ideas at the same time added to the excitement and risk of it all. According to Clodagh, everyone thought that they were crazy because it was such a risk, but Clodagh felt it was important for both her and her husband to explore their ideas while they had the chance (i.e. before the children started school and got settled in with friends, etc.). They both had great energy and felt that, with the work experience they had gained, they were at their peak.

Clodagh's husband had spoken to Enterprise Ireland[5] about his business idea and got an indication that he would be eligible for Cord[6] funding. This type of funding would be just the 'cushion' the couple needed. The markets were still feeling the effects of the September 11th tragedy and it was very quiet, not exactly the right time to start a new business. Even though it looked quite dismal at first, both Clodagh and her husband knew that things could only get better. They believed that with their experience, they were both highly employable.

Clodagh's website for her proposed service has been developed, although she has not yet sent it to a search engine. Despite the fact that she has not deliberately advertised the site, it is attracting attention through word of mouth, which is good for generating potential customers. At this early stage, the website, without the addresses and correcting service, is essentially a 'shop window' for her other programming/IT skills and services. This, at least, should help introduce her to the marketplace and build her reputation with potential future customers, all in preparation for her future service. In the meantime, Clodagh is branching out into website development, just to 'keep things ticking over'. She has spoken to the banks, as well as direct marketing companies, and offered them a trial. One of the banks came back to her and indicated that incorrect addressing was not really enough of a problem for them to worry about at present. This has led Clodagh to consider approaching ComReg and to work with them to do a countrywide address–correcting system.

During the past year, Clodagh has learned that banks would be unwilling to pay for a correcting system unnecessarily. In their view, there is already a system in place that they can rely on; in other words, the banks know that their post is going to get delivered at some point. So, while it does not seem to be enough of a problem for the banks at present, when incorrect addresses start to be redirected to other regions and simply left there for weeks, or until their addresses are corrected (which Clodagh feels will be the case), the situation might be viewed differently. It really is all a matter of timing as far as Clodagh is concerned and she needs to keep things ticking over in the meantime:

> I'm just developing websites to bide my time because I know (I hope) these changes will actually happen. So, it's all on the horizon

and in the meantime, I'm just doing enough to get by – yes, it's all a question of timing.

CLODAGH MALONE

DIFFICULTIES ENCOUNTERED

Clodagh has always been quite candid about the difficulties and barriers she encountered during the first twelve months of preparing to start-up her business. One of the main difficulties she identified was in relation to developing a customer base, which often required 'cold-calling'. This proved to be a huge learning curve for Clodagh and it took quite a while for her to gain confidence and get over her fear of saying the wrong thing or giving the wrong impression. Additionally, although she had significant contacts within the industry to help develop a customer base (having previously worked in the ICT sector), difficulties emerged around the whole issue of market credibility and the fact that the company was a start-up. For example, when Clodagh was telephoning people, even those with whom she had already made contact, she would often hear a different tone from them once she said she was starting up a business. Sometimes she felt a type of coldness, with the conversation not quite as cordial as normal. Even people she had worked with in the past and who knew her well appeared to be wary of a start-up. It was clear that potential customers were fearful of a small company – 'they wanted more weight behind it, they wanted advertising, they wanted six people to arrive at a meeting, to show that it was a big company – they needed to trust you'. In this regard, perseverance was fundamental. In Clodagh's view, if you are able to phone up a potential customer a few months after the initial contact, then that lends to your credibility – 'it shows you are still there, still plugging away, so, you must be serious'.

THE ISSUE OF GENDER

Clodagh's experiences were mixed when she considered the situation of being female in the ICT sector (traditionally a male-dominated sector). She felt that when making telephone calls to potential customers, she had to work harder to get her message across. Indeed, when she and her husband were making phone calls side by side, Clodagh felt that he was actually being listened to more. However, once credibility and trust were established, the issue of gender, whether perceived or real, was no longer a problem. Clodagh found that as soon as she would start to talk 'the jargon', or as soon as she told people about her experience, they seemed to respect her a bit more. Talking directly to people in their language, being able to listen and understand their problems and then talking to them about possible solutions, eliminated any gender differences. That said, however, Clodagh felt that the presence of her proposed business partner (who was male and in his fifties) at sales meetings was hugely important. According to Clodagh, the presence of a male business partner lent 'a bit of weight to the company'. This seemed to Clodagh to give both herself and her prospective customers more confidence.

SUPPORTS RECEIVED

In terms of the support Clodagh received in preparing to set up her business, participation on the North East Enterprise Platform Programme (NEEP[7]), a structured training programme for entrepreneurs in the ICT sector, was fundamental to the development of the business. Although having previously worked in the private sector and for two start-up enterprises, practical business experience, such as finance, accounting, marketing, selling and personal development, were important skills that Clodagh needed to develop. Participation on the NEEP programme provided the necessary training, skills development and support structures, at the right time, by the right people, at the right level. For example, the sales and marketing courses were held in the summer, which allowed the participants to 'get geared up again' for September, when everyone is typically back at work. For Clodagh, the personal development aspect of the training was simply life changing, even personality changing, because it changed her entire way of thinking. She began to stop looking inward and worrying about giving the right impression, adopting instead a more outward-looking philosophy. Now, whenever she meets new people, she listens to them and talks more about what *they* do rather than worrying about *herself*. One of the attractions of the NEEP programme for Clodagh was that it provided a range of business supports, including one-to-one business counselling; access to specialist training and consultancy services; access to resources, including incubation units, pilot plant and meeting facilities and access to a personal mentor under Enterprise Ireland's Mentor Programme. Having access to reputable accountants, legal advisors and professional sales and marketing people was invaluable for Clodagh.

FINANCIAL SUPPORTS

In addition to providing structured training, the NEEP participants also received financial support, which is crucial at the start-up stage. The financial support proved beneficial in a number of ways. In addition to providing a 'financial cushion', the programme, which was partly funded by Enterprise Ireland, gave credibility to the business idea. According to Clodagh, this is particularly important in Ireland, where referrals are an important aspect of everyday business practice. Once people heard that her idea was backed by Enterprise Ireland, they started to take her more seriously. Under the programme, participants are eligible for either financial support in the form of a grant of €550 per month or, subject to Enterprise Ireland's approval, additional funding in the form of a total package of 50 per cent of your verifiable salary (up to a maximum €38,000 − Cord funding) for one year. Clodagh was able to receive a grant of €550 per month.

NON-FINANCIAL SUPPORTS

Aside from the financial supports, the need for 'support' from family and friends was also vital. According to Clodagh, if you do not have this sort of support when you are trying to start a business, then 'you're finished'. Part of the reason for this is that the structured 9-to-5 format does not work well in a start-up situation. Everybody around you has to be flexible. The issue of family support was particularly pertinent in Clodagh's case, as her husband was also in a start-up situation.[8] This provided an element of companionship because they were both in 'the same boat'. However, this also meant that they were not as supportive of each other as they might have been. For example, Clodagh felt that she could not really expect her husband to give her support when he was trying to set up his business as well. There were times when his business idea would take priority and Clodagh's would have to fall back a little and vice versa. While on the one hand, they were both company for each other, on the other hand, Clodagh sometimes felt that the mutual support might be stronger if one of them was working full-time outside of the home rather than both of them trying to develop their own business.

Access to and contact with other start-up entrepreneurs were also considered important elements of the learning from the NEEP programme. In addition to the contact with the ten other aspiring entrepreneurs on the programme, which provided a useful mechanism to make new contacts and share experiences, access to shared office space, along with networking events, enhanced the learning from the programme. However, the fact that Clodagh was the only woman on the programme had its drawbacks. She indicated that it would have been great if there had been another female on the programme, just to compare notes and possibly to see if being in a relationship with family commitments, as opposed to being young, free and single, makes a difference to an aspiring female entrepreneur.

ADVICE FOR ASPIRING ENTREPRENEURS

Looking back over her experiences thus far, Clodagh adopts a very positive outlook. She stresses the importance of accountability – being accountable for her own actions and decisions – and her need for independence and control. By her own admission, she is not a patient person, so it was not surprising that the Public Sector, with its bureaucracy and red tape, did not suit her dynamic personality and drive. Like most entrepreneurs, Clodagh prefers things to move fast.

Focus was another key piece of advice Clodagh had to offer fellow aspiring entrepreneurs. According to Clodagh, if you wake up in the morning and do not really feel like doing something, then you know what is going to happen - you are not going to get anywhere. The preferred strategy is to do something, do anything. In Clodagh's view, even just making a few phone calls moves you along one step further. Indeed, every action will move an aspiring entrepreneur closer to their goal and that keeps the motivation levels up. Interestingly, for Clodagh, whenever she is working towards her own goals, the time seems to go by more quickly.

As previously highlighted in this case study, Clodagh viewed support from family and friends as critical in the pre-start-up phase and beyond. According to Clodagh, an aspiring entrepreneur needs to secure the support of their spouse, partner or parents before embarking on a proposed new business venture. In addition, having a plan 'B' in place ('just in case things don't work out according to plan') is an important consideration that will at least ensure you have something to fall back on. In this regard, Clodagh already had a plan B (developing websites on a consultancy basis), just, as she put it, 'to keep things ticking over'.

On a slightly more negative note, Clodagh admits that the entrepreneurial experience, even at the pre-start-up stage, can sometimes be terrifying. Sometimes it is easy to think that everyone wants the product and when they eventually say 'no', panic can set in. When what promised to be 'sure bets' turn out to be bitter disappointments, an aspiring entrepreneur can begin to wonder if there is any hope at all for their new idea. Interestingly, but not entirely surprising for this highly motivated, entrepreneurial individual, Clodagh has a tried-and-tested strategy for recovering from this sort of disappointment. She suggests that aspiring entrepreneurs try to get something out of their efforts, even if they have not managed to get the positive response for which they had hoped. Trying to get another name or contact who might be interested, or simply exploring other options, can lead on to all sorts of other possibilities.

Clodagh was successfully juggling family commitments with some consultancy projects that allowed her to work from home and generate a small revenue stream, while preparing to set up her own business. Although she had clearly experienced her ups and downs along the way and had still, by her own admission, a long way to go before she could reach set-up stage, she emphasised the need to maintain energy levels in relation to her entrepreneurial aspirations. For Clodagh, simply talking about a new idea too much could drain all its energy. For example, other people may not react in a positive way to a new idea or they may well be more enthusiastic about it, which in itself can drain energy away from an aspiring entrepreneur. Thus, Clodagh suggests that it is important to keep your idea to yourself to conserve its energy.

Clodagh's final piece of advice for those contemplating entrepreneurship was simple and to the point:

> Just do it - just make that phone call – don't wait for a moment that you think might be better, just do it! If you have a phone call to make or a hunch that trying something new might work – just do it – just try anything, operate outside your skin and just seize the day!

PROPOSED STRATEGY

Exploring the issue of business strategy and the future focus and direction of the business revealed a number of potential barriers to be overcome. One of the main themes to emerge in this respect was the fact that progress on the business idea was slower than initially anticipated. While Clodagh felt sure that things would have moved along much further at this stage, she was also aware that the failure of key market players to make a decision on postcoding had produced an obvious impact. Other unforeseen complications emerged due to the fact that Clodagh's proposed business partner has yet to retire from his full time job, thus adding a further delay to the project.

When asked about the long-term goals of the business, Clodagh was very excited about the future prospects, but stressed the need to ensure that the business remains manageable. She described the whole entrepreneurial process as both 'terrifying' and 'rewarding', and often worried about how she might cope with it all. While she had not specifically decided on how big the business would be, it was clear that, based on her own work experience, her preference was for a small business, with just the essential number of people:

> I would try to keep it fairly small – just the number of people I would absolutely need. So, I would say no more than 14 ... and it would be that high because of the labour intensive aspect of the business.

As she contemplates her proposed new business idea and moves closer to the set-up stage, it is clear that Clodagh still has a number of decisions to make. For example, one of her main concerns is how to generate revenues – will customers actually pay for the service or will the service be sponsored nationally, possibly by the state? What about customer requirements – who might use the service most? Will it appeal more to the private sector, including banks and marketing companies, rather than to individuals? Clodagh has really spent the last year trying to find the answers to such questions:

> ... it has been very much a searching sort of year – finding out what customers want, what type of customers would go for our services, who would pay; who cares about how the address looks on the envelope; who sends out enough post; who cares if the post doesn't get there the next day.

Despite such uncertainties, Clodagh still feels very positive about her proposed new business venture. However, with several issues facing her, she needs to decide what to do next. Concerns about intellectual property, for example, along with the business' apparent dependency on ComReg and An Post, will need to be addressed in order to move forward. On the one hand, there would appear to be a need for the technology Clodagh is developing. However, on the other hand, key players in the marketplace are yet to be convinced. While such delays in the introduction of new technologies are only to be expected, this in turn affects the overall pace at which Clodagh's proposed new business is developing. Should Clodagh simply develop her new technology independently, selling it off to large mail-shot/mail-order companies, rather than wait for commitments from key players? While this would help her to get established in the marketplace, such a decision would have obvious financial implications and Clodagh may need to start approaching potential investors to fund this approach. As Clodagh contemplates her future, it is clear that the next steps on her entrepreneurial journey are going to be crucial!

NOTES
1. This case is intended to be used as the basis for class discussion rather than to illustrate either effective or ineffective handling of a management situation.
2. Colette Henry is Head of the Department of Business Studies and Kate Johnston is Senior Researcher at the Centre for Entrepreneurship Research at the Dundalk Institute of Technology.
3. An Post is Ireland's state-owned national postal service.
4. For further details on the role and structure of ComReg, see www.comreg.ie
5. Enterprise Ireland is Ireland's state agency for the support and development of indigenous business.
6. Cord funding is state-awarded enterprise funding geared towards the commericalisation of research and development. It can provide financial support to the equivalent of up to 50 per cent of the promoter's previous salary.
7. This is a one-year full-time professional training and enterprise support programme which focuses on the needs of aspiring entrepreneurs with a well-thought-out, innovative business idea or technology that has the potential to be transformed into a high potential start-up company with export potential.
8. Clodagh's husband's proposed business was also in the ICT sector but targeting a different market.

3

General Records[1]

THOMAS M. COONEY[2]

Standing outside a pub, Billy Barrett and Martin Murphy faithfully obeyed the no smoking ban that was now a feature of the Irish social scene. As they smoked their cigarettes, they discussed the singer/songwriter who played inside the premises that they stood against so nonchalantly. The gig was enjoying a great reception, with the crowd enthusiastically applauding the eclectic mix of blues, rock, country and traditional music. 'Well, Billy, how would fancy starting a record company?' asked Martin, as if it were no big deal. 'The singer playing inside there wants to record an album but she has no label. I reckon that if we could put the money together, we could sign her up as our first artist and expand slowly as we learn about the industry. We could start it as a hobby and then see where it takes us. You never know, a few years from now we could be at the MTV Awards with our Acts performing on stage.' As Billy awoke gingerly the following morning after a late night of 'networking' as he termed it, he slowly recalled the previous evening and that he just might have agreed to start a record company.

DEVELOPING THE BUSINESS IDEA

A week later Billy and Martin met to discuss the reality of starting a record label. This time they met at Martin's home so that there would be no distractions. While it was an unusual prospect for both of them, there was a belief that if it was planned properly they really could make it work. They obviously could not compete directly against the major record labels so they needed to find an angle that would give them an advantage. They broadly agreed that the basic business concept being proposed was to form a record company that would limit the number of artists it signed but would work closely in partnership with them to enhance the prospect of the artist's success, thereby leading to a profitable existence for the record company. In its formative years, the company would seek to identify talented performers who believed in the philosophy of the organisation and were not mainstream in terms of their music, and to offer them a record deal for three albums. The company would focus on the production and marketing of CDs only, which would be sold through a variety of avenues. By specialising in particular segments of the music industry, providing individual attention to a small group of gifted clients, and niche marketing their material, Billy and Martin hoped to create a sustainable competitive advantage.

THE MUSIC INDUSTRY IN IRELAND

To help give them some idea of the industry in which they would be operating, Billy had undertaken some basic research to assess the size of the challenge that faced them. He was surprised to learn that there are over 100 record companies/distributors in Ireland, although the vast majority of them are small labels. There are also approximately 100 recording studios available for hire and approximately 20 CD manufacturers. In addition to these groups, there are also substantial groups of people working as sound engineers, producers, promoters, agents, A&R personnel, venue owners, publicists, publishers, graphic artists, printers, equipment manufacturers and an assortment of other personnel. However, the most frightening element from the information gathered centred around the issues of contracts and royalties. The music industry is renowned for legal cases arising from disputes over these issues and understanding the critical points of an artist's contract, a producer's contract and the computation of the various types of royalties was a legal nightmare for anyone new to the industry. The size and nature of the industry made Billy and Martin realise how little they actually knew about the music industry and how much they needed the help of someone on the inside.

MANAGEMENT TEAM

As Billy and Martin discussed their idea, they recognised that the first key area they needed to address was the management team. Martin (married with two young children) was a computer programmer who had an interest in music over many years. He was an accomplished singer and performed in chorals across the country. He had no experience of working in the music industry and had never been involved in recording music for an album. He worked as a freelance consultant and therefore had some understanding of the demands of setting up one's own business, even if it was not in the music industry. He was also a skilled negotiator and salesman. Because of his background, and also because it was his initiative that started the process, it was agreed that Martin would be CEO and would also take charge of operations.

Billy (single) worked for a training company delivering business management workshops but had little interest in music beyond buying some CDs. His knowledge of the music industry was practically zero but he had a passion for helping people to develop their business and wanted to see for himself what it was like to start a business. His particular expertise was in the area of marketing, so it made sense that he took responsibility for this area of the business. But they recognised that the team was weak in terms of industry experience and that they would need to bring other people on board quickly. To aid them in this process they identified the principal roles in the organisation and the key responsibilities of each role.

Billy and Martin both believed in the idea of building a strong team since the company would need a variety of strengths to get it established. They decided that on the next occasion they met they would compile a list of people whom they might approach to join them on their venture. If they were inviting people to join them, then they would also need to decide on how much equity they were willing to give up to attract the right people and finance.

MARKETING

Due to the career experiences of the management team, Billy and Martin recognised that the issue of marketing was crucial to the successful selling of any CD within the music industry and because they had limited funds they would need to generate a great deal of attention without spending much money. They decided that for the purposes of their first business plan, it was best to focus only on their first artist, rather than take a broad approach to their marketing strategy. The singer/songwriter whom they had enjoyed the evening that the idea of the record company was first suggested had verbally agreed to become the company's first artist. This artist had been a huge hit some years previously in Ireland but, having lived abroad for over a decade, she was now trying to re-establish herself in Ireland. She had been particularly successful among university students while based in Ireland and she would still receive requests from this group of fans asking where copies of her earlier albums could be purchased. Therefore it was decided to build a marketing plan for this first artist and, thereafter, each artist and CD would have individually tailored strategies devised for their needs rather than suggesting pre-determined models at this point.

Table 3.1: **Key Roles and Responsibilities**

CEO/Operations – Martin Murphy
- to direct strategic vision
- to co-ordinate activities
- to ensure the production of high quality products
- to organise logistics
- to represent the company in contractual talks
- to contract producer for each album.

Marketing – Billy Barrett
- to research and evaluate market opportunities
- to design marketing plans for each CD
- to oversee the promotional activities in appropriate markets
- to identify potential artists for the label
- to liaise with supporting alliances.

Finance
- to organise financial affairs
- to interact with financial institutions
- to present regular financial reports.

Industry Expert
- to provide advice on industry matters
- to proffer information which brings value to the company
- to initiate opportunities
- to introduce management team to industry personnel.

Non-Executive Advisors
- to bring relevant expertise to the company
- to offer advise and information.

TARGET CUSTOMERS

Based on the success of previous albums of the artist the target group was identified primarily as graduate students in Ireland over the past twenty years.

This group was central to the artist's previous success, as a base from which to build sales of this CD. The profile of the target group would be graduates aged between 25 and 40 with an appreciation for quality esoteric performers. Linked to this profile was a secondary group, that of existing third-level students. This decision was based on the principle of redeploying a formula that had already proved very successful for the artist in previous years. By engaging present-day students a new following could be developed, thus enlarging the overall fan base. Four geographic markets were identified for the first CD: Ireland, the internet, USA and Europe. Initially, Ireland and the internet were seen as the primary markets for this album.

1. Ireland – given the strength of the fan base in this country for this artist, the alliances with industry personnel, the ability to undertake a concert tour to launch the CD and the depth of knowledge presently held on that market made Ireland a strong launching base. However, it is also a very disparate market with few substantial niches and strong competition from the record companies, and from artists and groups trying to establish themselves. Thus, a focused promotional campaign would be essential to success and this would require hiring a specialist in promotional activity.

2. Internet – the second target market was based on the profile of the customer and the level of e-mail correspondence received by the artist. Consumer reports highlighted that the average user of the internet was more likely to be a well-educated urban dweller. General Records would design its own website that would allow people to order directly from the company, giving higher gross margins. The CD would be advertised on sites such as *The Irish Times on the Internet*, which attracts thousands of hits per day from the Irish abroad. Given the ability of exiled graduates to access such an avenue of distribution this represented an exciting opportunity to expand the traditional methods of selling the product. Other media used by exiled graduates would also be targeted.

The latter two were heavily dependent upon the success of these two markets and it was anticipated that sales in the European and American markets would initially come from off-stage sales. For this purpose the artist would be given the product at preferential terms and profits made thereafter would be allocated to her own accounts.

PRODUCT

In developing the product the company would be committed to a total quality product. While the music itself is central to a successful album, product enhancements also influence sales positively. The design of the cover would intensify the prospect of a sale and thus needed to be designed with great care and thought. Included within the sleeve notes would be the words of the songs, information on the website of the record label and of the artist, e-mail addresses to build a fan database so as to provide updated information, in addition to the data normally provided on the sleeve notes.

Following a number of phone calls placed in advance of the meeting, Martin and Billy had identified that the process involved appeared relatively straightforward. Having agreed a contract with the artist regarding the album, royalties and marketing activities, they would then need to identify a top-quality producer who would produce the album for them. They would also need to book a recording studio for a period of weeks, although many producers had their own studios. Once the album was finished it would need to be fine-tuned through mastering. The sleeve would need to be designed to fit the album and the target market before an independent company manufactured the completed sleeve. They would then need to have someone distribute the album to record stores throughout the country. Critical to the success of the album, they would need someone to generate hype for the album through radio play and the printed media. However simple it appeared, talking to people in the industry only highlighted the many challenges that awaited them.

DISTRIBUTION

Billy and Martin had readily decided that the CDs would be made available through distributors, direct sales from the company and direct sales from the artist. Each of these distribution avenues required a different approach and would need to be carefully researched.

1. Distributor – a distributor for Ireland had been proposed to Billy by someone that he knew in the business. The distribution fee was 25 per cent of the price to the distributor and payment on sales was made by them 45 days after the month of sales, less their 25 per cent. The company had the ability to make the product available nationwide, to provide support to the sales effort, to work within the overall strategy of the record label and within a cost structure that was agreeable to General Records. They also had the capacity to distribute in Europe should that

route be taken. A constant check would also be maintained on retail outlets to ensure every opportunity was available for people to purchase the album. The estimated sales from this source in the first three years of operation was 3,000 units. However, they would need to talk with other distributors first before making any decision on whom to employ.

2. Direct Sales from the Company – internet sales would be catered for by the company directly. As orders were received via the website the company would send a CD from its storage and mail it to the buyer. The buyer would carry the shipping costs. The estimated sales from this source in the first three years of operation was 1,000 units.

3. Direct Sales from the Artist – the company would sell the product in batch units to the artist at agreed terms. The artist would then be responsible for the sale of that inventory through live performances; 60 per cent of overall sales (i.e. 6,000 units) was anticipated to be sold via this channel of distribution in the first three years.

As the markets expanded, other forms of distribution would be considered and added to have the product as widely available as possible within the budget. It would be essential that each avenue be pursued vigorously so as to maximise sales for the company.

PROMOTION

A co-ordinated promotional campaign would be necessary to give maximum exposure to the launch of the album. This would involve interacting closely with the artist's promotional manager. Additionally, a professional music industry publicist would need to be hired to undertake the following activities:

*   Advertisements – on Hot Press and a select number of other media focused on the target market
*   Sponsorship – opportunities would be sought in which the album could be linked with sponsorship
*   TV Appearances – that the artist would appear on a minimum of three TV shows after the product launch
*   Radio – a co-ordinated campaign would 'plug' the album through complementary CDs to key DJs
*   Personal Selling – the directors would work with the publicist to promote the album intensively

- Notice Boards – much free publicity could be generated through the use of notice boards announcing events and music industry happenings
- PR – positive CD reviews would be vital to enhance the prospects of sales and thus a concentrated campaign would be made towards key individuals in the media.

This promotional campaign would be built around a concert tour at the time of launch although the company would not bear the costs of the tour.

MANUFACTURING
Four quotes had been received by telephone from Irish CD manufacturers in addition to an investigation of CD manufacturers in England. The best quote received was from a company in Dublin who offered a price of €2,500 per 1,000 CDs. This price included films, PQ encoding, glass mastering, four-page colour booklet, two-colour label, barcode and Gallup Chart registration. A number of options existed also to manufacture the product in America for the US and the internet markets. However, for the European market it would make more economic sense to manufacture the product in Ireland. All of these options needed further examination before a final decision could be made.

CD SLEEVE DESIGN
One Dublin design studio offered a design and print service based on they being supplied the artwork. The cost suggested was €1,500 for booklets, which would give full colour on pages one and four with text on pages two and three. Other design studios were also being investigated.

PRICING
As part of the preparations for the meeting, Martin had carried out some provisional research on what the cost might be for the album. These were only indicative figures but at least it gave them something to discuss before they examined the financial budgets in finer detail.

The following was the outline cost structure developed for the first album:

Initial Costs
- CD manufacturing = €7,500 (3,000 units x €2.50 per unit)
- Recording = €10,000

- Advance to artist = €2,500
- Other costs (including promotional activity, legal fees and general overheads) = €10,000
- Total = €30,000

Sales Prices
- To the artist for sales off-stage = €8
- To the distributor = €10
- To the consumer = €18

Royalties
- Mechanical/Publisher = 8 per cent of distributor's price (€0.80 per album but the company would seek a 50:50 split on these royalties)
- Artist = 7 per cent of distributor's price (€0.70 per album)
- Producer = 3 per cent of distributor's price (€0.30 per album)
- Public performance/Broadcasting = this is calculated depending on usage and goes to the publishers of the songs.

The amount paid for the royalties on each album would remain the same for each avenue of distribution. These figures were not exact but a detailed computation of the figures was proving difficult at this point due to the need for negotiation on mechanical/publishing royalties, artist royalties, producer royalties and broadcasting royalties. These royalties would also be influenced by performance and by a tiered financial arrangement that the company hoped to put in place with the artist. However, the principal argument from Martin and Billy's perspective was that each contract would be negotiated to recoup the investment as quickly as possible.

FINANCING THE COMPANY

A key difficulty that any start-up faces is how to finance the operation. Billy and Martin discussed at length the various options that were open to them. Between them they could raise about €10,000, with Martin putting in €6,000 for 60 per cent of the company and Billy getting 40 per cent for his €4,000. That still left them €20,000 short. As they would get no grant aid for this type of business, that meant that they would have to raise €20,000 either through loan finance or through equity finance. They perceived that a bank would be slow to offer a loan to this type of business given the difficult market in which it would be operating. It also made little sense for a professional investor to put money into the company as they suspected that the potential return on investment would be low, although they could not be sure of this until the financial budgets had been completed. Billy suggested that they should seek finance from their friends who might be interested in the venture for what he termed 'cocktail party value', that is the ability to tell friends and work colleagues that you have a piece of action in a record company which Billy hoped might attract some of their friends who had cash to spare.

GETTING LATE

It was now 2a.m. and Billy and Martin were beginning to tire. They had got through a significant amount of work but many decisions remained outstanding. For example, they would need to develop a more detailed marketing strategy, especially if they were looking to develop the business beyond the first album. Instead of looking at the business as one album, maybe they should take a more professional approach and develop a detailed business plan for the company. They really had no vision of where they wanted the company to be in three years' time. They also needed to consider what type of people they should bring onto their management team and what they could offer them in return. Contract and royalty negotiations would be critical and they had no experience in this area. Most of all they needed to develop detailed financial calculations to give themselves a break-even figure and expected rates of return. The most difficult question of all was what business proposition were they going to offer the potential investors that they needed to get the company started and what would be the exit strategy for the investors. As Billy headed for the front door, he turned to Martin and quietly asked, 'Are we mad?'

NOTES

1. This case is intended to be used as the basis for class discussion rather than to illustrate either effective or ineffective handling of a management situation.
2. Thomas M. Cooney is a Lecturer in Entrepreneurship at the Dublin Institute of Technology.

4
Philip Kenny Designs[1]

CONOR CARROLL and MARK O'CONNELL[2]

It is late February and Philip Kenny has just returned to his studio in Limerick from his latest visit to the Frankfurt trade show. At the show Philip received a lot of very positive feedback about his designs. He also spotted a number of opportunities that he had previously never explored. It was the first time one of his colleagues accompanied him to the trade show and what they witnessed at the show gave Philip, fresh drive and enthusiasm for the business that he has built from scratch.

Philip is a well-known Irish designer based in Limerick, where he designs and produces an exclusive range of tableware and giftware. These products are made to Philip's individual designs from a combination of ceramic, wood, metal and plastics. The business has had its fair share of success and setbacks, yet this entrepreneur has been unrelenting in his pursuit of success with his design products. His company has been and is facing a barrage of difficulties, strong competitors using celebrity endorsements, manufacturing capacity problems, outsourcing conundrums, restricted cash flow and limited ability to raise additional capital. As Philip turned on the lights of his premises on a dreary, wet Monday and looked into the workspace, he thought, 'Where do I go from here? What will deliver the success I have always believed existed for this business?'

BACKGROUND
Philip started out on his entrepreneurial adventure as a graduate of Industrial Design, a joint degree programme between the University of Limerick and the National College of Art and Design, Dublin. Originally from Dublin, he studied pottery and ceramics, his main interest, before eventually switching to Industrial Design. After graduating, he went to work for a firm specialising in the design of waste management systems for

Third World countries. He was exposed to the design of these systems and learned about the interaction between design and manufacturing. After this experience he moved back to Limerick, as his wife was from the area.

At this time a fellow graduate of the Industrial Design programme had set up a successful design consultancy based in the university campus Innovation Centre. This company sold design services to other campus companies and factories. Philip joined him and worked there for three years before leaving to establish his own practice design consultancy. He set up his own consultancy, called 'Blackbox Ltd', specialising in tableware and homeware, where he felt he was getting back to his original interest in pottery. The firm grew to employ nine staff, providing a range of services from product design to graphic design. The firm's main customer was the Birmingham based Swan Industries, which was taken over by French multinational Moulineux. In 1991, at the height of the recession in Ireland, providing design services proved unsustainable and he decided to sell the business with a view to getting involved in freelance consultancy. His former employer placed an offer for Blackbox, thereby buying out Philip. Six weeks later the company who had bought him out went bust!

By this time Philip had already started his consulting business and was concurrently developing a product range. Philip managed a few clients as a freelance consultant while simultaneously developing prototype tableware products from his shed at home with a view to launching them onto the Irish market. He manufactured small runs of product until eventually he gained enough confidence in his products to start up his own brand. He subsequently launched these products under the brand name 'Tableart'. As part of his strategy to get Tableart established he took on a number of agency roles for a range of knives, peppermills and tableware. This way he could boost the product range that he was selling to potential customers. His underlying strategy was to establish himself primarily as a housewares agent and then introduce his own product line into the channel. At the same time he was able to learn about buyers and pricing strategies for these types of products and markets.

After becoming more familiar with the homewares marketplace, Philip became acutely aware of the importance of branding. Having taken advice from a marketing consultant, he set about changing the branding of his products to communicate a quality product range positioned at the higher end of the market. He realised that people bought into the idea of well-designed, crafted products and that having a well-recognised brand name was essential to achieving success. As a result he tested numerous brand identities and decided on his signature design concept – 'Philip Kenny Contemporary Design'. He found that he had to tie the product with the maker and create a designer brand name in order to be successful. The signature range was the way forward based on market acceptance of other signature ranges in the gift and houseware segments (for example Stephen Pearce, Nicholas Moss).

I realised that to compete effectively in this sector and to achieve the market position necessary for success, it was essential to connect the product with me directly through personal branding.

PHILIP KENNY

Table 4.1: **Philip Kenny Studio – At a Glance**

Background of Philip Kenny
- Industrial Design Graduate
- Gained commercial experience working in manufacturing industry
- Moved back to Limerick. Set up a successful design consultancy
- Sold consultancy to competitor
- From his shed he created prototype Homeware products
- Had a premises in the Temple Bar, Dublin for a period of time
- Now has Design studio, where he designs and manufactures a variety of Homeware products for stores such as Brown Thomas and Harvey Nichols
- He is doing extra work in terms of consultancy and lecturing in industrial design.

Location of Studio
Clondrinagh Business Park, Ennis Road, Limerick

Types of Products Sold	Competitor Brands
Bread Bins, Cheese Platters, Chopping Boards, Fish Platter, Tea Warmer, Teapot, Food Warmer, Relish Set, Store Jars, Salad Bowl, Salad Server, Lazy Susan Set, Coaster Set, Trivet, Spice Set, Serving Trays and Lumens	Bodum Nigella Lawson's 'Living Kitchenware' T&G Woodware Typhoon

DEVELOPING THE PRODUCT RANGE

The inspiration for his product range did not come simply from his creativity and strong design talent. He decided at an early stage that he had to design products that were low in tooling cost and high on added value. As a result he selected materials such as wood, ceramics and metal that are amenable to low entry cost in terms of tooling and set up. He visited numerous international tradeshows (such as 'Exclusively Homewares' and 'Top Drawer' in London, 'Ambiente' in Frankfurt and the 'Birmingham Spring Fair'), undertaking extensive research in the area of housewares products. By doing so he kept abreast of changing trends in the industry, gained ideas and saw products that inspired him to make different variations of product concepts.

Philip then started by going through his design stage, prototyping varying product concepts. By the end of this period he had eight products designed, all based on the ceramic, metal and wood theme, and all using contemporary modern influences. His initial business concept was to outsource the manufacture of these products and to concentrate on product development of the range, his core skill. During the product design process, he had learned what was difficult and costly to produce. At this stage he realised that huge problems could arise due to quality and cost issues. Outsourcing meant that the quality was not always in Philip's control, particularly when sourcing supplies in locations as diverse as from Stoke to Poland.

Apart from the issue of quality control, which was crucial to consolidating Philip Kenny Contemporary Designs premium market position, he was also faced with volume difficulties. In order to outsource effectively, suppliers wanted large orders to make it viable for them to supply to Ireland. These suppliers request minimum order quantities running into thousands. The cost saved by using these suppliers is very significant, but scale is the issue[3]. Buying such large quantities would then lead to other difficulties in terms of cash flow management and simple logistical problems such as where to store the thousands of units required.

STARTING OUT

Philip initially exhibited at numerous trade shows and took substantial orders from interested companies for his product range. However, due to outsourcing problems, he often had to write to customers saying that an order was delayed, or that particular items in the range could not be delivered. This situation was totally unsatisfactory from everyone's perspective. Something had to change! During this time he was still operating part-time, doing freelance consultancy and working from his shed at home assembling the products. Eventually Philip made the fundamental choice to change the business. He had taken a year out to reassess the situation, deciding not to take any new orders, finish all his outstanding orders and clear all debts. The following year an opportunity arose in Dublin's Temple Bar, where he was invited to be part of a co-operative, a direct selling craft venture in the area managed by TBP (Temple Bar Proprieties). TBP sold the proposition to a number of other budding entrepreneurs of fitting out a building and getting small craft and design businesses to sell their produce from this shop. Philip thought it was a good idea, based on the prime location of the property. He decided to take a licence for six months and try it out. As part of the process in changing the business and committing himself fully, he re-mortgaged his house, bought wood-working machinery and began to supply his newly fitted-out retail unit.

The shop worked well for the first three months, due to a sponsored radio and television advertising campaign. Once the advertising ended sales collapsed and he decided that the Dublin venture was not viable in the long term due to the uncertainty that existed about the future of the store. He decided not to renew his rental licence in the property. He returned to Limerick and continued working on his product range on a stop-start basis. He now felt despondent as he was continuing to experience outsourcing problems. A key outsourced ceramic supplier closed, adding further to the pressure that he was enduring. On particular days, he felt like quitting, thinking that the business would not work, until he would suddenly be boosted by a significant order. Despite the supply difficulties he realised that he had a good product that people wanted. He needed to rethink his business process and develop a new strategy. Central to this strategy was the need to acquire a key customer. This relationship would leverage business from smaller operators once they saw the brand being stocked by leading retailers. He felt that this association with an established retailer would act as a badge of approval.

As part of the overall strategy he set out his operational and marketing objectives. He needed a suitable manufacturing base in Limerick that could cope with the anticipated growth. He also recognised that he could no longer operate alone and needed to bring in someone to work with him. He hired a graduate from the Industrial Design course who would have exposure to design and manufacture. He took up a lease on a property operated in an incubation unit. He had the base and the staff, now all he needed were customers! This fundamental decision to source stand-alone premises transformed his outlook from viewing the enterprise as being a small pet project to a real business that needed 100 per cent commitment.

Philip always acknowledged that his cash flow did not allow him to engage in the type of marketing and branding exercises that his competitors undertake with the luxury of large marketing budgets. He always knew he would have to engage in clever and tactical marketing that would reap high dividends with low cash input. A high profile retailer was the priority for Philip, more specifically Brown Thomas, one of Ireland's most successful department store chains. It was the perfect fit for the Philip Kenny product range – exclusive, high end and expensive. Brown Thomas were also keen to source a product range in the upper price category which was not well represented in the store by other suppliers. As part of the trading agreement, Brown Thomas sought exclusivity. Philip agreed to supply Brown Thomas on an exclusive basis a new range of products that he was developing, but only for a certain period of time. An extensive product range was developed and Brown Thomas placed an order for the equivalent of €32,000.

Philip believed that this order was now going to set the business in motion. It was not significant in terms of profit, but it had good potential for ongoing orders. This could also lead to other retailers being interested in the product range. Again outsourcing problems arose from a new ceramic supplier, who failed to meet their supply commitment, due to their priorities to larger customers. This led to Philip only being able to fill three quarters of the initial Brown Thomas order. All of the non-ceramic products were supplied to Brown Thomas but there were shortages due to the lack of ceramic components. In the meantime, the products that were supplied were selling fast and new orders came in from Brown Thomas stores nationwide. However, Philip was going to have increased difficulty meeting these new orders due to his ongoing supply problems. At the start of the exclusive distribution arrangement, the Philip Kenny range was stocked in prime store locations. However, as new products ranges came in, the stock was moved around to store space that did not have the same impact as the prime sites. The Philip Kenny Design range was now at the mercy of the store and department managers.

Despite the product range selling very well, in the New Year the Brown Thomas buyer decided not to renew any more orders with Philip Kenny.

This was a major setback and he had to rethink his strategy, yet again. However, he leveraged this link with Brown Thomas to try to gain access to other UK multiples such as the House of Fraser, a prestigious department store chain. He continued to receive a lot of interest in the product, yet still had supply concerns. He was worried that the supply issues would adversely affect the brand from the perspective of the retailers. In the meantime he was still supplying his old range, but with the end of the arrangement with Brown Thomas he was now free to extend the new product collections to all customers, once he could supply them.

THE PRODUCT STRATEGY

The Philip Kenny brand is designed to exude 'contemporary, modern, clean lines and simplicity'. Many customers view his designs as very Scandinavian in style. The product range totals about twenty items, ranging from chopping boards to storage jars. His trade customers usually buy relatively small quantities of the products, typically single figures for particular types of products. On average the value of the orders would be small, varying between €300 and €1,500. A lot of trade customers are craft shops, even though the product is not strictly classified as a craft product. The busiest time of the year is March, when orders are placed. This is because of the company's trade show activity in January and February.[4] If orders are not placed at these shows, they start to come in through customer follow up. Goods are usually delivered from May with a rush in September and October for the Christmas season.

A challenge that Philip Kenny faces is that his product designs are not patentable. For a small firm the cost of patenting every design is prohibitive and very hard to enforce. Typically if he launches a new design at a trade show it is possible that a variation of the product will be in a competitor's portfolio within a year. However, if somebody creates an absolute copy of a product there is recourse for the designer. Philip is a member of ACID (Anti Copying in Design), which is a design insurance scheme. If an exact copy is spotted, a person can contact this organisation and from there ACID will have their legal team issue a cease and desist order or seek compensation for the infringement. It costs approximately €250 a year to be a member of ACID.

Due to the nature of the designs and the number of components per item he designs, Philip has no choice but to outsource as manufacturing costs in Ireland increase. He still has ambitions to buy his own ceramic kiln to manufacture some of the ceramic components and to have more control over this element of production. Although he does not want to outsource completely, because of bad past experiences, he wants to reduce his reliance on outside suppliers. With his team of advisors, they attempted to evaluate the business following what they witnessed at trade shows. Based on their experiences at the show they decided to adopt a new two-part strategy focusing on product creation and to rebrand the business to reflect an even more personally driven brand. They felt that they needed some products that would be easier to make and to build on the product range. They decided they would focus on developing expensive pieces and small fast movers, impulse purchases (for example wooden bookmarks for €2.95). These kinds of products could go into totally different types of stores, such as newsagents, bookstores, etc. By adopting this strategy he felt he would further utilise his machinery and work using waste materials from other wooden products. These smaller products would also be branded as from the Philip Kenny Studio.

The second part of their new business strategy was that 'Philip Kenny Homewares' needed to refocus more on the design of products. With that in mind he changed the brand to 'Philip Kenny Design Studio'. The concept behind the studio brand is that the Philip Kenny identity would continue to represent the brand while each item created would be credited to whatever designer actually worked on the piece, a similar idea that is used in furniture stores such as Habitat or Ikea – 'designed by (name of designer)'. In this way all of the products would be personalised as having being designed by a particular designer. The concept is to have a brochure with a variety of products under the Philip Kenny Studio Brand with a wide collection of products, design being the driving force, ranging from homewares to small impulse buys. The aim is to focus on creating a design brand. He has already received a lot of interest in these types of products from corporate gift companies and even wedding list retailers.

> The Philip Kenny signature logo makes a huge difference to people. It seems to really matter to them.
>
> PHILIP KENNY

As part of his focus on the design brand, he is working with a number of young designers who are interested in making products at his design studio. Philip feels these young designers do not have an opportunity to make products. He also allows these designers to use his studio to work on their own projects. Included among the designers are individuals with ceramic and wood experience, which fits in well with the products Philip Kenny has produced. He envisions that his studio will become a creative hub for young designers, providing them with an opportunity to manufacture and to commercialise their work.

Initially, Philip experimented with selling products at his shop that would complement his range, such as candles. However, the local county council served Philip with a warning and threatened him with a €12,000 order fine for breach of planning laws. Faced with this threat, Philip now only sells his own products that are made on the premises. The other materials are just used as 'props' to showcase his products in an appropriate setting. The studio is now a factory outlet and contributes a welcome cash flow for Philip.

CUSTOMERS

The vast majority of Philip Kenny's customers are female. The age profile is 25 years and upwards. The market is divided into products that are bought as gifts or as self-purchases. Gift purchases for weddings are very popular while corporate gifts are a growing segment also. In addition, special contracts are carried out for firms (for example, the company supplied the new Crowne Plaza Hotel in Dublin with accessories). The price of the product at retail level is 2.5 times the trade price. Philip feels that the changeover to the euro (€) has made items appear to be more expensive. However his customers are attracted to high quality products rather than run-of-the-mill-type products.

> Nothing goes out of here without the Philip Kenny badge on it.
> PHILIP KENNY

MARKETING STRATEGY

By his own admission there is no marketing plan that he follows. The strategy is *ad hoc* rather than planned. This is due to more pressing calls on his budgets. He uses trade shows as both a primary research mechanism to see what competitors are offering and the main mechanism used to attract trade customers. These events are very useful in that they bring together, in a single location, a group of distributors and customers. Also, they help Philip identify sales leads, service current accounts and reinforce relationships with these retailers. He also has the opportunity to gather competitor information, assess new ideas and ultimately sell the product.

Apart from trade shows, 'shoe leather marketing' is his most effective strategy. He has found that cold calling is a very effective sales tool due to the impact and strength of his product range. Originally he never thought of doing cold calling to potential customers due to the time constraints that he was under. However, a friend of Philip's convinced him that he needed to get into the car and call to potential customers. Every week he came back with an order. The strength of the product really opened doors for him.

The company has no marketing budget. Philip realises that the brand is not in the public eye. It is a testament to the strength of the product that orders keep coming. The company does not have a salesperson. He feels that the company could do well with even as little as €1,000 a month spent on advertising in a magazine publication, coupled with trade shows and cold calling. The company has done a small bit of publicity, receiving coverage in the local papers from two separate features. Even this small-scale activity has had a direct impact on sales. The company does not have a website (it did have a website initially, but the company could not use a site for direct sales because of a lack of necessary infrastructure).

Overall he recognises that marketing is a major weakness in the company but time and money prevent him from tackling his immediate competitors head on through promotion. Instead he must market cleverly using the resources he has. The decision to reposition the brand as a design studio will have marketing implications in terms of communicating the uniqueness of the approach. However, without the benefit of a marketing budget he must continue to rely on trade shows and customer contact to convey the new direction of the design studio concept. In addition he must market the new range of 'impulse' purchases compounding the range of product development and promotional issues that he has to contend with in realising his new business model.

MAIN COMPETITORS

Philip Kenny faces a number of key competitors. Bodum (Danish company) has fifty-two stores, a presence in fourteen different countries and designs a wide range of homeware items from kettles to chopping boards. Bodum has developed a really strong product range. It presents the same quality offering as Philip Kenny.

Typhoon, a successful British company, outsources the manufacturing of all its products from the Far East. It has taken on a very ethnic feel for its product range, which includes sushi dishes and rice bowls. Their price point is half that of the Philip Kenny's product range. However, his range of products is perceived as higher in quality – and 'looks the money'. These competitors have significant advantages over Philip Kenny Design, especially in the areas of size and scale. Their products can be sourced at a much cheaper price and they can fulfil large orders for multiples. Furthermore, they have excellent distribution networks and large sales teams working in the industry, vying for business.

Table 4.2: **Main Competitors at a Glance**

BODUM	T&G WOODWARE	TYPHOON	NIGELLA LAWSON'S LIVING KITCHENWARE
Based in Denmark	Based in the UK	Based in the UK	Based in the UK
Product range is very varied and includes coffee jugs, coffee makers, large woodware collection, kitchen utensils, etc.	Product range includes chopping boards, pepper mills, trolleys, wine racks and a variety of assorted product.	Product range is very varied and includes kitchen utensils, weighing scales, large woodware collection, large ceramics collection, gadgets, etc.	Product range includes bread bins, storage jars, chopping boards, mixing bowls and other kitchen gadgets.
Runs a network of Bodum branded shops and supplies major department stores and independent cookery stores. Possesses very large product portfolio. Utilises a network of agents, distributors and wholly owned subsidiaries for its export markets.	Strong competitor competing at a lower price points. Supplies all the major department stores and independent cookery stores. Over 700 product lines. Uses pine and beechwood extensively. Works with low-profile celebrity chefs. Utilises a network of agents and distributors for its export markets.	Has a strong Asian ethnic theme in its design. Supplies all the major department stores and independent cookery stores. Possesses huge product portfolio. Utilises graphite, wood, ceramic and stainless steel. Uses Gary Rhodes as a celebrity endorser. Has a presence in over 28 different countries.	Created in conjunction with Sebastian Conran. Very successful brand, with a comparable product range to Philip Kenny Designs. Strong influence of white and aqua blue colours in product range. Available in major department stores such as Debenhams, Selfridges, etc. Has distribution coverage in the US, Canada, Australia and New Zealand.

In addition, celebrity brands (such as Nigella Lawson's 'Living Kitchenware' and others such as Jamie Oliver) are a major threat to the Philip Kenny brand, in that they provide direct competition. Their products are directly comparable to the Philip Kenny range. Nigella Lawson, the celebrity chef and lifestyle guru, has partnered with Sebastian Conran (son of designer Terence Conran) and InterDesign to launch Nigella's 'Living Kitchen Collection', a range of homeware. Celebrity brands have had an enormous impact on this product category, with numerous celebrities linking up with manufacturers. Jamie Oliver has a branding arrangement with fine cookware and tableware maker Royal Worcester. Celebrity brands also include people such as Lloyd Grossman, Anthony Worral Thompson and Gary Rhodes. These celebrities are highly marketable brands, providing their endorsed product with huge recognition and favourable attitudes and represent a huge threat for a small business trying to grow. However, the 'Philip Kenny Design' brand strength is that it can sell at the high end to a number of specialist shops.

Other competitors specialise in a particular product category, like chopping boards and bread bins, but the Philip Kenny range differs significantly from these in that it combines different types of material such as wood, metal and ceramic (for example T&G Woodware).

THE NEXT STEP

Philip Kenny has numerous problems facing his business including mounting competition, supply problems, stretched financing, branding issues and even Nigella Lawson! Faced with these huge threats, he has a lot of tough decisions to make. More innovation is required in terms of developing low-cost products to manufacture. Philip Kenny would like to grow the business, which to date has become his passion, but he knows he has to change the way in which the business operates. He also knows that he has a great product that is in demand with both consumers and retailers alike. But what strategies need to be adopted in order to take the business forward into the future?

NOTES

1. This case is intended to be used as the basis for class discussion rather than to illustrate either effective or ineffective handling of a management situation.
2. Conor Carroll is a Lecturer in Marketing at the University of Limerick. Mark O'Connell is a Director of BDO Simpson Xavier, Limerick.
3. For example, the company sources spice jars for US$3.00 each, yet these can be sourced in the Far East for US 0.63c. However, this supplier requests a minimum order quantity of 10,000 units.
4. The 'Maison et Object' in Paris and 'Showcase' in London is in late January. 'Birmingham Spring Fair' and 'Frankfurt Show' is in February.

5

RealFoodatHome[1]

RealFoodatHome is a gourmet meal delivery service founded in 2001 by Fabrizio Memon. Fabrizio came up with the idea for the business while a student in the MBA program at the University College Dublin (UCD) Smurfit School of Business and formed the company in partnership with Chef Neil McFadden and Chef Ray O'Haire. The concept for the company was based on the founders' own experiences of living busy lives and having little time or energy at the end of the day to come home and cook an interesting, healthy and tasty meal. The founders realised that they probably were not alone. A little research showed that compared to a few years ago, people are indeed working longer, more stressful days and commuting further distances. In Dublin, daily commutes to the office can commonly take from 30 minutes to more than an hour each way.

The founders noted that they and people they knew enjoyed eating good meals, but instead of cooking healthy and tasty dinners, often resorted to quick and convenient meals such as pasta, hamburgers or take-away food. Cooking a full meal took too long at the end of the day and felt like a chore. They decided what was needed was a service that offered pre-prepared, delicious gourmet meals that could easily be cooked at the end of a hectic day. What was neede was RealFoodatHome.

The company's value proposition to customers is simple. It offers busy people the ability to cook a delicious gourmet meal in their own homes in less than 30 minutes. It eliminates the hassle of supermarket shopping for ingredients, and the time and drudgery of prep work, while preserving the joy of eating delicious good food.

THE PRODUCT

The RealFoodatHome product is a pre-prepared dinner 'kit'. A kit contains all the food and ingredients for a gourmet dinner for two people. Most kits include a starter, such as a salad or soup, which is almost ready to eat and can be prepared to serve in just a few minutes. The main course can be prepared to serve in about twenty minutes. The kits include a description of each course and its ingredients and instructions on how to prepare them at home (see an example in Appendix 5.1).

RealFoodatHome's pre-prepared dinners provide customers:

- An interesting and healthy dinner menu
- All ingredients assembled and pre-measured (except salt and water)
- All the prep work, such as peeling potatoes, marinating meat and chopping vegetables, completed.

There is a strong focus within the company on offering high quality and local ingredients. Irish beef, pork and lamb are always used, and fish dishes are made from fresh fish caught in Irish waters. The company audits and visits its suppliers, including farmers, to assure compliance with high standards of production. Irish vegetables, potatoes and other produce are used if possible, so most dishes are created according to seasonal availability. There are no preservatives used in RealFoodatHome dinners, so the kits must be refrigerated through to the time of cooking and must be consumed within a few days. The company makes kits each morning and delivers them every day to ensure freshness.

How it Works

The RealFoodatHome kits are easy to order and have delivered. Customers simply call RealFoodatHome or go online to www.realfoodathome.com to select from one of three dinner menus that are available weekly. The menus are created by RealFoodatHome chefs based on seasonality and availability of ingredients. Once the dinner menu is selected, customers also have the option to order wine and dessert to complement their meal.

RealFoodatHome kits can be ordered as late as 3p.m. for same-day delivery by 5:30p.m., or customers have the option to pre-order for later in the week. Once ordered, the kit can be delivered by refrigerated vans to a variety of office locations in Dublin city centre. The company maintains branded refrigerators at Accenture, Esat BT, Oracle and Price WaterhouseCoopers, but will also deliver to most other office locations in Dublin city centre. It makes limited home deliveries to customers in Dublin 2, 3, 4 and 15. For customers in the broader Dublin metro area, the company makes deliveries to O'Brien's wine stores in Blackrock, Donnybrook, Malahide, Rathmines and Sandymount. The meals are refrigerated in the O'Brien's fridges for customers to collect at the end of the day. The RealFoodatHome vans also carry extra meals so that even if the 3p.m. order time has passed, they may be able to fulfil orders made later in the afternoon. For the truly spontaneous, another option is to pick up a kit that does not have to be pre-ordered, from either O'Brien's wines in Donnybrook or the third floor of Brown Thomas on Grafton Street.

MANAGEMENT TEAM

The company has three full-time directors that make up the core management team:

Fabrizio Memon is the managing director of RealFoodatHome. In 1998 he started his own consultancy business in Sales Coaching, which leveraged his experience in sales. After determining that the consultancy business could not reach sufficient scale, Fabrizio began searching for something else to do. He then enrolled in the one-year MBA at the Smurfit School where he founded RealFoodatHome.

Neil McFadden is a partner and director of RealFoodatHome and one of the chefs. Neil completed his culinary training at the Dublin College of Catering, with an apprenticeship in Ernie's of Donnybrook. He spent several years training and cooking in Switzerland and Belgium and then returned to Dublin. Before joining RealFoodatHome, Neil was the Executive Chef at Luttrelstown Castle.

Ray O'Haire is a partner and director of RealFoodatHome and one of the chefs. Ray obtained his culinary and academic training in Ireland and overseas and spent three years working in Longueville Manor Hotel, Jersey. He returned to Ireland in 1997 and was the head chef of Campbell Catering before joining RealFoodatHome.

The company is aware that it needs to round out its management team by hiring a marketing director, a personal assistant for the managing director and a chief operating officer. To date the company has not been able to afford hiring additional personnel based on their current and projected cash flow.

CUSTOMERS

Since the RealFoodatHome website went live in August 2002, the company has attracted several hundred customers. Many customers are busy working couples or families who order from RealFoodatHome on a regular basis one or more times per month. Others have identified RealFoodatHome as an alternative to hiring caterers and order deliveries for mid-week dinner parties and get-togethers with friends. RealFoodatHome also does a brisk business over bank holiday weekends and during holidays and special occasions, when it attracts customers who are planning to entertain friends and family. Many of these orders are larger – for six people or more. For instance, over the summer RealFoodatHome introduced a Barbecue Party kit that contains Kerry sirloin steak, cajun chicken, Hicks sausages, baking potatoes, salads, garlic bread and dessert. The kit is priced at €150 and will feed 10 to 12 people.

The company stays in contact with its customers on a weekly basis through e-mail. Each Monday it e-mails the dinner menus available that week and sends a catchy follow-up e-mail near the end of the week to encourage Friday and weekend orders. Customers have the option to 'unsubscribe' from these e-mails, but the unsubscribe rate to date has been negligible.

PRICING

The company's pricing strategy is to keep the per person costs of its dinners low enough to attract casual diners that would normally opt for take-away. Its current maximum price point of €14 per person is set to attract a wide range of customers. Kits for two people that include a starter and a main course are priced up to €28. Kits without a starter can be priced as low as €9 per person, or €18 per kit.

THE COMPETITION

While there is not a direct competitor that offers the same services as RealFoodatHome in Ireland, there is still significant competition from other dining options such as restaurants and take-away.

RealFoodatHome's competitive positioning is to offer the quality of restaurant dining but with the convenience and price of take-away, as Table 5.1 illustrates.

Table 5.1: **Competitors at a Glance**

	Quality Food	Convenience	Time Savings	Price
RealFoodatHome	High	High	High	Low
Home cooking	High	Low	Low	Low
Prepared supermarket food	Medium	High	Medium	Low
Take-away	Medium	High	High	Medium
Restaurants	High	High	High	High
Caterers	High	High	High	High

FINANCIALS

While growing at an impressive year-over-year rate, RealFoodatHome revenues are still modest in scale. The company's revenues and projections, which do not include any additional financing, are:

Table 5.2: **RealFoodatHome Revenue Projections**

	2002(A)	2003(A)	2004(P)	2005(P)	2007(P)
Revenues (000's)	€100	€200	€500	€850	€1,100
Net Income	Negative	Negative	Negative	Negative	Profitable

Note: (A) is actual figures and (P) are projected.

The company's revenues are quite seasonal. During most of the year, they have sales of approximately €20,000 per month. December represents the peak of business as customers place large orders for holiday entertaining. In 2003, the company earned about €100,000 in revenues for December, which is the equivalent of four to five months of average revenues. The company currently has five employees, but brings on as many as ten people around the peak holiday season of Christmas. A part-time marketing person is in the process of being hired.

EXIT STRATEGY

The likely exit for an investor in this company is an acquisition from a larger food services company in Ireland or England. A supermarket such as SuperQuinn or Marks & Spencer could develop an interest in providing high-end ready-to-cook meals through their existing stores and become a potential acquirer of RealFoodatHome.

FINANCING

RealFoodatHome has raised a total of €310,000 in equity financing from outside investors and about €100,000 from the company's directors, as summarised below. The company is currently contemplating an additional round of financing between €500,000 and €2 million.

Table 5.3: **RealFoodatHome Financing History**

Year	Source	Financing raised
2001	Founders	€92,000
2002	Friends and Family	€60,000
2002	Dublin City Enterprise Board	€50,000
2003	Leading Irish Bank	€250,000
TOTAL		**€452,000**

The company initially began operating while Fabrizio was a student at the Smurfit School at UCD, which allowed him to take advantage of the NovaUCD's 2002 Campus Company Development Programme. As a UCD campus company, RealFoodatHome could avail of on–campus facilities, faculty and support to develop the business plan, obtain advice and seek financing. In its early stages, the company was financed by €92,000 invested by the founders and €60,000 raised from five friends of Fabrizio. In 2002, the Dublin County Enterprise Board invested €50,000 in debt finance at a 5 per cent interest rate. The company can pay off this debt with no penalty. The Enterprise Board also has an option to convert the debt to equity at any time if it chooses.

Last year, RealFoodatHome raised its first professional round of financing from a leading Irish bank. The bank invested €250,000, of which the company net €215,000 after transaction costs. The bank obtained 35 per cent of the company in that round of financing, which indicates a valuation of about €700,000. The company planned to use the proceeds from the financing to marketing, expand to service areas outside Dublin city centre and improve the user experience on the company website. To date, the company has completed all those objectives.

Since obtaining financing, the company has made significant strides by:

- Obtaining press in the form of favourable reviews in all the major Irish newspapers, conducting some limited marketing through Enterprise Board speaking engagements and UCD interviews
- Expanding services to areas outside Dublin 2 by implementing an agreement with O'Brien's wines for delivery of RealFoodatHome kits
- Re-launching the company's website to include a more sophisticated look and feel and an easier and more reliable ordering process.

The company has also expanded its product offerings to include 'family pack' kits, frequent ethnic and vegetarian offerings and lower priced meals that provide only a main course, without a starter.

Future Strategy

The management team is currently contemplating an additional round of financing between €500,000 and €2 million in order to:

- Hire a marketing person and increase the marketing budget significantly in order to grow the customer base
- Hire an assistant for the managing director
- Make improvements to the cooking/production facility in order to support future growth. The company currently produces its meals at Coolmine Industrial Park in Clonsilla, Dublin 15. Depending on how much additional capital is raised, the company could make improvements to the existing facility, or lease a larger, more sophisticated kitchen elsewhere.

The company is currently in discussions with its advisors about its future, its capital needs and the possibilities of another round of financing. The team has not yet determined how much money to raise or from where to raise it (for example from a group of angel investors, from VCs or from debt financing). The existing VC has indicated that they are no longer making small venture investments, so they will not be participating in any further rounds of financing.

A number of key issues related to the fundraising must be considered, including dilution of ownership by the management team, valuation expectations and to what inflection point the financing should get the company. To successfully achieve the next stage of growth and ultimately an attractive exit for investors, the company must decide upon a financing strategy that takes all of these issues into consideration.

NOTES

1. This case is intended to be used as the basis for class discussion rather than to illustrate either effective or ineffective handling of a management situation.
2. Diane Mulcahy was a Visiting Research Fellow at the Policy Institute at Trinity College, Dublin (2003/2004).

Appendix 5.1

An example of the RealFoodatHome dinner menu options for one week

Healthy and Tasty (€28 per kit):
Starter
A fresh salad of mixed leaves, crisp bacon, grated beetroot and croutons with balsamic vinaigrette

Main Course
Tender marinated lamb steaks with new potatoes, roast root vegetables and red wine sauce

Thai Special (€28 per kit):
Starter
Skewer of tender chicken with Thai spice, served with separate peanut sauce

Main Course
Tender Kerry beef, stir-fried with ginger, Thai sauce and broccoli, served with aromatic rice

ReatFoodatHome Lite (€18 per kit):
Starter
There is no Starter with this menu

Main Course
Penne with a sauce of smoked bacon, plum tomatoes and fresh basil leaves with handmade garlic bread

6

Turner Print Group[1]

PHILIP McGOVERN[2]

I n Ireland, the print and packaging industry is comprised of about 900 indigenous and foreign-owned companies. Many sub-sectors fall under this category including corrugated cases, labels, cartons, magazine and newspaper printing, computer manual services, book printing and paper sacks. The industry also provides key support for many of Ireland's vital hi-tech industrial sectors such as communications, information technology, pharmaceuticals, food and engineering.

Historically, the print and packaging industry has maintained a high level of flexibility in response to changing market conditions and technological innovations. The printing techniques of today are more environmentally friendly than ever before, producing less waste paper and less waste ink. Over the past two decades, web-offset printing of newspaper and digital print media have become the industry standard throughout Ireland. The driving technology within the industry is the offset press. Irish magazine printers use MAN Roland, KBA and Harris high-speed machines, while carton and book printers rely on Heidelberg and Komori presses.

According to the Irish Printing Federation (IPF), a significant amount of rationalisation has been ongoing in the industry. While there were no large-scale job losses in 2003, many companies have shed between five and ten jobs each. Kevin Walsh, president of the IPF, believes that over-capacity is only part of the problem. 'Softening in demand and decreases in margins are piling on the pressure,' he said. Desktop publishing is now a low-cost business and this is eating into the traditional printing business with ever-decreasing dependency on traditional printing craft skills. The structure of many print firm operations is still based on the anachronistic practices of the old crafts which have become obsolete. Traditionally, printing was seen as a prestigious craft business. Printers were highly skilled and served a five-year apprenticeship before attaining the status of 'master craftsman', which practically guaranteed a highly-paid job for life. Declining orders and rising costs (including increased labour costs) now bedevil the printing sector. Walsh also pointed out that the printing industry in Ireland is largely dependent upon the home market but due to the bulk of many printed items exports are generally not economically viable. Yet, imports of printed material into the Republic from elsewhere in the EU and from Asia are building steadily and are currently worth around €330 million annually. For the first time ever, imports are now worth as much as exports. Walsh argues that difficulties remain in getting government support for the industry while in other EU countries there is a high level of support. As an example, he cited the annual book fair in Frankfurt in 2003, the most important meeting place for the world's book publishers, where the Canadians had fifteen stands and Canada, as a result, was 'terrifically branded' as a publishing and printing country. In contrast, there was no branding for Ireland and promotional support did not extend much beyond a free calendar provided by the industry itself (See Appendix 6.1(a) and 6.1(b)).

CHANGE IN THE PRINT INDUSTRY

Apart from the economic impact of the high tech slowdown, as well as the slackening demand from other sectors of the economy, the key driver in the printing industry is technical change. Run lengths are reducing all the time, as clients want literature on a Just-in-Time (JIT) basis so that they can reduce their storage costs to a minimum. Faster turnaround times are needed and this, together with short lead times, means that printing equipment manufacturers are under considerable pressure to innovate constantly and help printing firms reduce costs. More automation is also demanded so that printers can reduce the time that it takes to switch from one job to the next. Some companies have introduced touch screen technology on all of their presses, which helps speed up the setting of ink ducts, register and formats. Production integration is increasing so that pre-press machines, such as image setters, plate setters and scanners, can 'talk' to presses even faster and more accurately than before. It is now much easier to store information about jobs so that when the time comes for reruns, the set-up time is greatly reduced. Other new technologies are also making an impact, such as direct imaging, which merges pre-press and press into one operation by imaging the plate in place on the press.

Most core processes are currently digitalised, particularly the pre-press stages. With the increasing trend towards digital printing, successful printers are expanding their services and looking for new markets. Print companies are gradually becoming total solution providers, not just providers of print. Customer needs are constantly changing, driven by factors such as globalisation, outsourcing by large companies and e-commerce. Technological innovations are continually being introduced resulting in updates throughout all aspects of the business, including print production systems, print products and even in the industry's basic structure. Changes in the media and telecommunications sectors have also trickled down to affect the print industry, as evidenced by reduced set-up times and increased output.

Meanwhile, developments in digital technology have been an asset to the printing industry. New opportunities have opened up for mass customisation, direct mail and other promotional materials as a result of these developments. The industry has responded deftly by seizing emerging business opportunities. Some of these include niche areas within the sector in print management, logistics and public procurement outsourcing. These areas help companies create a strong competitive advantage. Another avenue of opportunity lies within the computer manual business. Investment and changes in operations within this business are providing new and necessary services. A significant export business has also built up around the label industry based on service and quality – the pharmaceutical industry in particular has inspired high specification print and packaging requirements.

COMPANY BACKGROUND

A history of one company exemplifies the constant struggle to adapt and survive. The Turner Print Group has a long tradition with many of the family descendants involved in the craft from the early 18th century. In the early 1930s, Harold and Eric Turner, great grandsons of Robert Turner, (Printer and Publisher of the *Leitrim Advertiser* from 1849), took over the helm of the family print business in Longford. Their expertise and knowledge of the business and their commitment to investing in new technology has so far enabled the company to survive and prosper. This continuous development over the years has ensured that the company ranks as one of Ireland's foremost printing houses. Now the fifth generation of the Turner family, brothers Warren (managing director) and Derick (operations director) have further developed and expanded the business, creating Turner Print Group – a leading name in the printing industry.

DEVELOPMENTS

The Print Room in the Turner Print Group has the latest generation of presses and operates 24 hours each day to meet customers' requirements. The press managers are continually briefed with advancements in changing technology and improvements in printing methods and standards. Many options are available to customers with a complete range of Heidelberg multi-colour presses – from single colour B3 with numbering and perforating to B3, B2 and B1 four colour and B1 six colour. The range of equipment allows considerable flexibility, thus ensuring all print requirements are produced to requisite deadlines and within cost estimates.

A wide variety of services are available to suit a broad customer spectrum. Specialised punching exists for the food, beverage and pharmaceutical industries. Many options exist for laminating, cutting and folding. The pressroom includes single colour to ten colour machines with 24-hour shifts which ensures the customer has many options. The work produced covers many sectors, including tourist guides, semi-state publications, company stationery, annual reports, promotional material, books, magazines and material for a number of financial organisations. Products are produced confidentially to meet customers' requirements with delivery dates to internationally recognised quality standards.

Despite pressure from cheaper rivals in the UK, speed and reliability are the strengths on which Turner Print Group thrives. 'Our aim is to compete with the best in Europe,' says Warren Turner (managing director), who joined the firm as a management trainee in the early 1970s.

> Advances in technology have enhanced efficiency levels, which has enabled us to compete effectively in the single currency marketplace. As well as losing business because of price, it is difficult to plan investment because we have to compete on an equal basis with the policies and practices in place in other European countries.

However, the company recognises the reality of the European marketplace. 'I have heard public representatives say Irish businesses are not lean enough but I defy them to find fault with our efficiency. We have made huge changes to compete and now produce 70 per cent more than ten years ago, while employing 15 per cent fewer people,' says Derick, who heads up operations and production.

Innovation is one thing the company has never feared, even in 1836 when the company was founded by Robert Turner, a printer of repute. 'We always invest in the latest and best equipment on the market,' says Warren. In his time the firm has gone from hot-metal presses to digital technology.

> Our new kit, which takes type from computer straight to print, is ground-breaking and the way of the future because it enables us to print on demand and makes shorter print-runs viable, allowing the company to move on from economy of scale considerations. We are able to invest heavily because we are a private company with the major shareholders – the Turner family – giving emphasis to reinvestment in the medium term.

In recent years the company spent in excess of €12 million on new technology, which has positioned the firm at the forefront of the printing industry in Ireland. This allows the company to think medium-term by avoiding the necessity to maintain a high dividend to keep investors satisfied.

Advances in technology also mean that the factory is not the noisy place that one would expect. These days there is no hard manual labour, nor drops of ink on the concrete floor. The efficiencies gained by each investment have helped the firm achieve environmental recognition. As technology has advanced, so too has the capacity that the Turner Print Group can handle. Five years ago its printing machinery produced 3,000 sheets per hour – these days it can do more than quadruple that. A wide range of specialised finishing equipment complements the press room.

Traditionally, the company's busiest time is the three months up to Christmas. Spare capacity in the first part of the year has led the firm to look for other work, namely company reports. It produces work for many of the country's leading financial, publishing and industrial organisations. It has recently secured a further four-year contract to produce stationery requirements for a leading financial institution, which has greatly boosted the firm's reputation in the financial services sector. This new side of the business – a market worth €40 million – should help the company achieve its 2004 sales target of €10 million, with profits of €300,000 compared with last year's €200,000 (see Appendix 6.2 and 6.3). A number of small acquisitions since the 1990s have allowed the company to provide a greater range of services, including picture scanning, web design and websites. Warren acknowledges that acquiring a manufacturing base on the continent may be necessary in the future to maintain cost-effective manufacturing output. In the Northern Ireland market, the company's reputation for quality and delivery has allowed it to charge a premium over its competitors. Warren affirms that it is important that they retain this reputation for quality and that they are fortunate to have considerable talent coming up through the company. 'People are crucial to the company's success,' he says. That is the reason why the company, which now employs 67 people, has been thinking ahead about how it can retain good staff. 'We have a great team, are fully unionised and try to involve everyone in decision-making. Remuneration and bonuses are a key feature, but we are finding it more difficult to keep what is effectively a manufacturing job attractive to young people,' says Warren.

Over time, the cost and quality advantages of Digital Print Technology, together with its ability to produce multiple copies at high speed, make it the dominant technology, and with it the Turner Print Group's model of centralised printing, the industry norm. This business concept of centralised printing required a set of capabilities that the Turner Print Group developed and which, in turn, served as its major strengths and as key barriers to entry to the business. Given the advantages of volume and speed, large organisations find centralised printing highly attractive and they become the key customers for high quality design and print. In order to support this corporate customer base, the Turner Print Group's product designs and upgrades emphasise economies of higher volume printing. To market its products effectively, the Turner Print Group also built up an extensive direct sales and customer service organisation. Account executives spend a considerable amount of time ensuring that customers have a 'trouble free' experience. The company has built limited design capabilities for market customisation and simultaneously maintained high levels of investment in both technology and manufacturing to support its growing market. It continues to spend in excess of €10,000 a year in Marketing/R&D.

COMPETITION

The nature of the competition is changing dramatically for the company. In the 1990s, competition threatened from a number of Dublin-based companies. This was managed effectively as the Turner Print Group's cost base was lower (Longford location) than their competitors. Since then, however, competition has emerged from a number of new directions including:

1. Newspaper companies that have invested in state of the art computerised printing facilities leave them with spare capacity which allows them to price work at a marginal cost
2. Competition from outside Ireland, as far as Eastern Europe and beyond – this is a serious long-term problem as labour costs are significantly

lower and the increased delivery times is not a limiting factor in most cases.

One of the challenges facing the company is how to meet these new competitive threats.

CAPABILITY BUILDING

The Turner Print Group is admired for its technical innovation, marketing expertise and low-cost quality manufacturing. These are the result of a medium-term strategy to become a premier print organisation. The company has frequently acquired outside expertise so that it could better focus internal investments on skills of strategic importance. This approach of extensive outsourcing and focused internal development has required consistent direction from senior management and the patience to allow the firm to become well grounded in one skill area before taxing the organisation with the next objective.

The Turner Print Group perceives technology as an enabler for increasing efficiency and improving work practices and as a crucial link in the communications channel between the customer and the supplier. According to Warren, a company that increases its dependency on technology – whether it is hardware, e-mail or the myriad of financial software programs available – must be prepared for the demands that this increased reliance will place on its business processes. For some firms technology can be a double-edged sword, since it not only brings competitive advantage, it is also brings many pitfalls. According to Warren, a clear message has been broadcast to the industry over the past five years – either automate or liquidate.

TECHNOLOGY

The company's many innovative products, which enabled it to grow quickly in the 1980s and 1990s, are in large part the result of the carefully orchestrated use of technology and this has generated the capacity for managing rapid technological change. Attesting to its prolific output of original designs is the fact that the Turner Print Group have been among the leaders in the industry throughout the 1990s. According to Derick, 'considerable investment is going into Computer to Plate (CtP) systems, while print management are looking very carefully at workflow situations, not just for the printing presses, but also for the whole production processes'. One of the prime considerations for the firm is getting colour consistency on presses as quickly as possible and minimising the number of waste sheets. Previously, getting the settings correct to produce the right colours meant wasting hundreds of sheets of paper; modern day make-ready techniques mean that now only a few sheets are needed. However, the Turner Print Group acknowledges that it has neither the resources nor the time to develop all necessary technologies and has therefore frequently traded or bought specific technologies from a variety of external partners.

The company also recognises that its continued market success depends on its ability to quickly exploit new research into marketable products. Over the past five years, the company has strategically set out to reduce new product introduction cycle time through cross-functional integration and World Class Manufacturing (WCM), whose purpose is to cut development time by 30 per cent on a continuous basis. The main trust of this programme is the classification of development projects by total time required and the critical human resources needed so that these two parameters can be optimised for each product depending on its importance for the Turner Print Group's entrepreneurial strategy. This allows product teams to be formed around several classifications of product development priorities of which 'best sellers' will receive the most emphasis. These are the products aimed at new markets or segments with large potential demands. Other classifications include products necessary to catch up with competitive offerings, product refinements intended to enhance customer satisfaction and long-run marathon products, which will take considerable time to develop. The company emphasises three factors to reduce time to market: fostering of production ability, efficient technical support systems and careful reviews of product development at all stages. The Turner Print Group is also working to divert its traditional product focus into more of a market focus. To this end, its production staff participate in product strategy meetings, carry out consumer research, join in marketing activities and attend meetings in the field of domestic and foreign sales outlets.

MANUFACTURING

The Turner Print Group's goal in manufacturing is to produce the best quality at the lowest cost with on-time delivery. To drive cost down, a key philosophy of the production system is to organise the production of each product run so that the minimum amount of time, energy and resources are required. It places a strong emphasis on tight inventory management through a stable production planning process, careful material planning, close supplier relationships and adherence to a Just-in-Time (JIT) system of inventory movement. A formal waste elimination programme continues to add value to the company, with plans to install ISO 14001 in the near future. 'This commitment reinforces our drive to ensure we are always meeting environmental responsibilities for our customers, suppliers and staff,' says Warren. Overall, the company accomplished a 13 per cent rise in productivity per year from 1996 to 2003 through automation and innovative process improvements.

Although management and staff readily acknowledge the importance of metrics and information flow, measuring performances – beyond basic financial indicators – rarely occurs in the company. The constraints of not having a measuring system can best be summed up by one of the company's managers: 'For example, we couldn't give you a figure on what proportion of our print jobs are in progress (according to any agreed delivery schedule) because we do not have readily accessible reports generated by (any) system. We also need to do more to improve the tracking of materials through the factory.'

Cognisant of this, the company is in the process of installing a computerised warehouse management system which will allow inventory management to be automated and up-to-date information to be available to hand on any stock movements. The warehouse facility can accommodate 1,500 euro pallets. This system will allow the operators to have up-to-the-minute live information in relation to product by part, quality and location and allow them to pick products based on the first-in-first-out (FIFO) system. The inventory system will also be completely integrated into the main frame manufacturing system. Distribution is handled through the firm's transport department along with the assistance of strategic logistics partnerships.

The workforce is held in high regard in the Turner Print Group. A philosophy of 'stop and fix it' empowers any worker to stop the production line if they are not able to perform a task properly or if they observe a quality problem. Production staff are responsible for their own machine maintenance governed by rules which stress prevention. Targets for quality and production, and other critical data, are presented to the workers with online feedback. Most workers participate in voluntary 'small group activity' for problem solving. The result of these practices is a workforce that feels individually responsible for the success of the products that it manufactures.

The company has additionally been able to demonstrate milestone achievements – potential investors require it to demonstrate that it has a history of delivering against plans and that there is a 'real' future market for products. 'Making sales alone will not have much impact on our bottom line unless we actually collect the cash from customers in a timely manner. In order to do this, we need to ensure that we have adequate controls in place over the collection of amounts due,' Warren states. There is an appointed person whose role is to follow up on amounts due. Where amounts have not been settled by the invoice due date, a phone call is made to customers as a reminder. Based on the outcome of this, credit information on existing customers is updated. Customers are monitored regularly, watching for early signs of trouble. Where appropriate, sales staff are involved in these collection efforts.

The Turner Print Group sponsor a highly regarded suggestion programme for its staff in order to directly involve those most familiar with the work processes in improving the business. The programme was originally initiated in 1987 with only limited success, but in the early 1990s, participation soared with more than thirty suggestions per employee per year. All suggestions are reviewed by a committee. The quality and effectiveness of the process was demonstrated by an 80 per cent implementation rate of the suggestions offered and corporate savings of €20,000 in the year 2002. This process also has the additional benefit of empowering employees to identify areas that require improvement in the organisation and enabling them to feel part of the decision-making process in the company.

LEVERAGING EXPERTISE

The Turner Print Group places critical importance on continued growth through diversification into new product fields. Whenever the company introduced a new product, profits surged forward. Whenever innovation lagged, so did the earnings. In order to survive in the current era of extreme competition, management believes that it must possess at least five proprietary state-of-the-art products at any one time that will enable it to develop unique customer segments. The personal qualities required to drive growth are just as important as finance. A manager needs belief and commitment, with the awareness to recognise opportunity, the experience to assess it accurately and the courage to see it through. Management believes that a company must be ready to change and adapt, while holding true to its core values.

The company has chosen to integrate backward only on parts with unique technologies. For other components, it prefers to develop long-term relationships with its suppliers and to retain two sources for most parts. The company maintains its own in-house capability for doing pilot production to understand better the technology and the vendors' costs. Delegation is also considered very important, as an entrepreneur cannot have all the relevant skills and qualities to grow the business, certainly not after the initial stages. Management believes that it is the collective qualities of the management team that has been responsible for the continuing success of the organisation.

Diversification has always been important to the Turner Print Group in order to further its growth. In 1995, a new fulfilment services unit was established to explore the fields of customised printing (i.e. turnkey operations). While an avid supporter of diversification, Warren was also cautious. In order to ensure the enduring survival of The Turner Print Group, they consider that they have to continue diversifying in order to adapt to environmental changes, while minimising the risks involved. It is estimated that entering a new business which requires either a technology unrelated to the Turner Print Group's expertise or a different marketing channel than the group currently uses incurs a 40 per cent risk. If the company attempts to enter a new business that requires both a new technology and a new marketing channel that they are unfamiliar with, then the risk entailed in such ventures would be adjudged to be 100 per cent. There are two prerequisites that have to be satisfied before launching such new ventures. First, the operation must be debt-free; second, they will able to secure the staff capable of competently undertaking such ventures.

COMBINING CAPABILITIES

Through its R&D strategy, the Turner Print Group has worked to build up specialised expertise in several areas and link them to other state of the art print products. Through the 1980s and 1990s it focused on products related to its main business and expertise – magazine printing. This prompted the introduction of continuous printing – focusing on turnkey operations. There was minimal risk because the printing technology was the same and the market outlet remained the same. However, entry into the financial services market pushed the Turner Print Group into developing expertise in the field of CtP, which it later combined with web-based capability to introduce one of its most successful products, website online printing. The company is now seriously committed to R&D in web-based printing because its vision foresees the arrival of on-demand printing as flexible on-demand printing is dictating radical change which will lend itself to further development of web-based technological know-how.

CREATIVE DESTRUCTION

New ideas in engineering are changing the way that machines are designed and consequently posing major threats to traditional finishing departments. At the same time, advances in information technology are linking stitchers, binders and folders into data networks, while automated set-ups and console controls are allowing for remote management and are removing much of the operating burden from staff. The greatest impact on the Turner Print Group for the foreseeable future is going to come from Job Definition Format (JDF), end-to-end production data formatting which is finding widespread acceptance in print areas. The idea of JDF is that if the format of a brochure or catalogue is known during the creation phases, the information can be used to preset machinery that is going to be used to produce it, thereby saving manufacturing time. Crucially, as all the dimensions are set at an early phase, there will be no need to enter these figures again, so errors through miss-keying data will be avoided.

A second aspect to JDF is that information about performance and progress will be gathered and retrieved from a central point or made available to a customer. Production scheduling and costing will become more accurate and customer relationships will be deepened. This underlying Schumpeterian philosophy implies that costs will be reduced because advances in technological knowledge will enable new production processes to be used that should be cheaper than the old processes, thereby stimulating innovation in new products and new processes. The challenge for the Turner Print Group will be to link these discrete technologies, so that the print provider and buyer integrate new internet processes with their own relevant business processes to prevent unnecessary multiple data inputs into systems. This aspiration should further contribute to an optimised workflow, lead to shorter cycle times and ultimately lower costs via integrated procurement processes.

Supporting this history of exploiting capabilities to create new products and work practices, lies a unique management process. The company has institutionalised corporate entrepreneurship through its autonomous market-focused business structure. There is a senior management group, which provides the bridge between the entrepreneurial business functions and the company's key capabilities in manufacturing, technology and market awareness.

Warren feels that there are four basic requirements for the success of a print business: competence in the development of new product offerings;

quality, low-cost manufacturing technology; marketing strength; and brand identity. He has established a steering group to address these four requirements with the following objectives:

- To foster the creation of new product technology applications by continuously improving the development process
- To achieve optimum quality by minimising waste in all areas of manufacturing
- To strengthen the company's brand identity by building a quality service and professional sales support staff.

While it has been a relatively simple process to identify the basic requirements and objectives for the organisation, planning how to make them happen has proved far more challenging.

MARKETING

The pressure to deliver newer, faster, more streamlined products to customers, makes old-style marketing skills a basic requirement, not a differentiating one, for any marketing person in the organisation. Such elemental skills are considered necessary but not sufficient for business success. Increased competition, quality and cut-throat competitive pricing no longer differentiate print products - something else is required. If a customer can buy a product from many different companies that are indistinguishable in price and quality, how are they going to choose? Business must change its thinking about the complexity and nature of the person making purchasing decisions. So, it is not sufficient to give customers choice – choice has to be embedded in security and combined with a sense of empowerment.

These points refer only to the customer. What about the people who actually produce, finish, market and deliver the print products? How about the management team who are creating the overall business strategy – how are they managing the change process? There is little point in developing a sophisticated profile of customer/potential customer needs, if getting the company to change and innovate is like trying to get the Titanic to do a u-turn.

The marketing strategy of the Turner Print Group has been the result of step-by-step, calculated introduction strategies. Typically, the product is first introduced and perfected in-house before ever being sold on the consumer market. Additionally, by the early 1990s, the Group had built up a strong customer network that was supported by sales and service staff. The company continued to enthusiastically support the user network and felt that a close relationship with its customers was a vital asset that allowed it to understand and react to user needs in a timely manner. However, over the past five years, many print managers have become frustrated that 'marketing does not seem to be working any more'. Companies are finding it harder to connect with customers. Customer relationship management (CRM) systems that promised so much appear to have delivered very little in this industry. The conventional tools and techniques of marketing no longer appear to be relevant. Added to this, marketing's contribution to the print business is constantly under question. In effect, the certainties of the marketing environment have been replaced with the uncertainties of a dynamically complex marketplace.

The print sector itself has gone through more change in one decade than in the previous century. This change, and its effects, is still occurring and the industry has to accept the new reality of continuous change. Almost imperceptibly, the economic plates are shifting, sending tremors through the players and re-arranging a landscape that had appeared so static and immovable for so long. Equilibrium is being replaced with a state of continual change and uncertainty. In a variety of small ways, the fault lines are emerging with sudden clarity; there is movement from a production-driven to consumption-led economy, where the nature of the exchange is different and this difference is exacerbated by the force of the internet and e-commerce. In the wake of this shift, a number of challenges have arisen in the marketing of a print service.

There is the need to embrace a new kind of consumer, one that has variously been described as 'active', 'knowledgeable' and 'post-modern'. In essence this is a New Consumer, a creature distinctly different and identifiable from its predecessors. For this New Consumer time is a precious commodity in lives that are becoming increasingly complex. In their purchasing behaviour, New Consumers now look for brand 'experiences' over and above bundles of features and benefits. They are more IT enabled and marketing orientated than ever before. New consumers inhabit an interactive marketplace that is characterised by high levels of heterogeneity that dispute the assumptions of conventional marketing thinking. The Turner Print Group is aiming to respond to this new consumer grouping and this means focusing on the demand side of their businesses – doing the same thing better or doing something new. To achieve this, it needs to connect better with customers and understand how to deliver value that customers are seeking in a continually adaptive and innovative way.

Criticism about the lack of clarity surrounding marketing's contribution to the print business has been a feature of reports and articles over recent years. This is partly driven by the difficulties surrounding the measurement of marketing effectiveness, but also by the fact that marketing is both equated with business strategy and located within the marketing mix. Without a clear emphasis as to its role, marketing languishes in a 'no-mans-land' and arguably is badly placed to provide strategic leadership.

CHALLENGES

Meeting the challenges identified by management requires a different way of conceptualising the marketing process and a different approach to implementation. The Turner Print Group is looking for strategies that will enable it to survive in the face of continual change (i.e. establishing proprietary positions in the marketplace and tailoring products to the special needs of each segment). Does the solution lie in adopting a value-centric orientation within the business, or will this in turn re-invent the role of service? Table 6.1 shows how the practice of marketing in the Turner Print Group has evolved in response to market conditions and how the underlying philosophy of the business in relation to the customers it serves has shifted.

Table 6.1: Evolution of Marketing in the Turner Print Group

Focus	Means	End
Sales orientation	Transaction marketing	Profits through acquiring customers
Retention orientation	Customer relationship management	Profits through customer satisfaction
Value orientation	Demand print management	Profits through insight, innovation and agility

Transaction marketing was based on a sales orientation with the aim of acquiring as many new customers as possible. Profit was generated through increased sales volume. Marketing then switched emphasis to developing greater profitability through customer satisfaction, underpinned by a retention orientation. The realities of a consumer-led economy demand that the focus of a print business shifts to customer responsiveness – based on superior processes of insight, innovation and agility – to achieve profitability. This means replacing the focus on customer retention with a value-centric orientation. Value-centric orientation means delivering value that customers want to buy into and the firm wants to deliver, i.e. value on the customers' terms – demanded and perhaps dictated by them. This value component marks the process of exchange that takes place between the customer and the organisation – it is the 'thing' that the customer gets in turn for what they give. It means moving beyond a relationship emphasis to one of value creation. If the Turner Print Group can meet the value expectations of the customer, then a long-term and profitable relationship is more likely to follow. 'We try to ensure that our staff have character and go out of their way to help customers,' says Warren. The key to achieving this is to have value as the starting point – otherwise the relationship development strategy will not work as intended.

The arrival of the customer-led economy has elevated the role of service in the creation and delivery of the print value proposition. Increasingly, the Turner Print Group is recognising service as a source of competitive advantage. The customers' experience of the brand is delivered through the actions and attitudes of staff. In effect, the service delivered by staff is the brand. The objective is to get employees to live the brand, as they are the people through whom customers experience the brand. The Turner Print Group develops strategy as it goes along (emergent). It is very close to the market and is able to expose itself to high levels of risk successfully because it knows what its customers want instinctively and it can change more quickly than competitors.

MANAGING RENEWAL

An established business like the Turner Print Group has to strive to stay ahead of competition, through diversification, competitive intelligence or the ability to adapt to changes in the market by repositioning its brand. Warren asserts that this will involve a root-and-branch re-examination of the company's brand proposition – perhaps even necessitating the development of a new brand logo or symbol. This will mean an analysis of what it is that differentiates their products from what their competitors offer, using this as a starting-point to begin a fresh assault on the market. There is a risk that some of their core products become commodities and there are competitors in the market that are trying to change the rules of the game. The main objective for the company is to continually earn profits on a stable basis to ensure survival. To implement this goal, they must diversify. According to the managing director, such aspirations require the company to build up the ability to absorb temporary upheavals without panic – aspiration without stability makes the company lose its way. While celebrating the company's past successes, Warren constantly reminds his colleagues that no organisational form or process holds the eternal truth. The need to change within a changing world is inevitable:

> In the future, our main efforts must be concentrated on clearly defining and differentiating the markets of the respective products and creating appropriate marketing solutions for them. In order to make this a reality, we may have to combine our field sales operation with the in-house marketing and sales support functions to fully meet market needs.

The Turner Print Group realise that to survive they need to be competitive, not just by Irish standards but by global ones as this is the market within which they operate.

NOTES

1. This case is intended to be used as the basis for class discussion rather than to illustrate either effective or ineffective handling of a management situation.
2. Philip McGovern is a Lecturer in Management at the Institute of Technology, Tallaght.

Appendix 6.1(a): **Gross Output versus All Manufacturing**

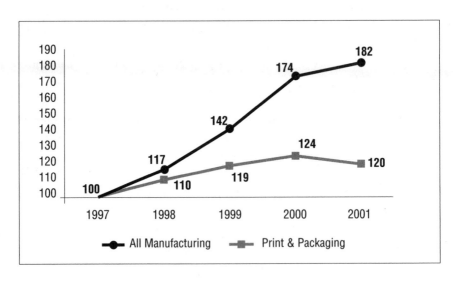

Source: Central Statistics Office Estimate 2004

Appendix 6.1(b): **Net Output versus All Manufacturing**

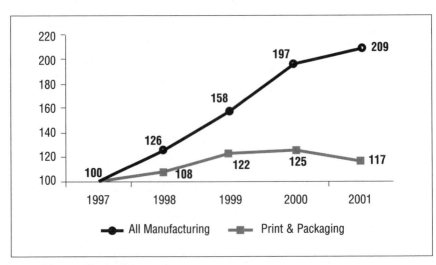

Source: Central Statistics Office Estimate 2004

Note: Gross output represents the value of goods sold. Net output excludes the value of materials and other inputs into the manufacturing process. The net output measure indicates the value added by the printing industry.

Appendix 6.2: **Prospects for Turner Print Group**

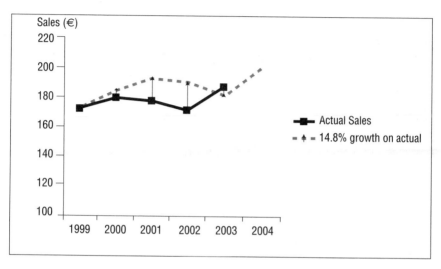

Source: Company Estimates

Appendix 6.3: **Five Year Financial Summary**

	1999 €	2000 €	2001 €	2002 €	2003 €
Net Sales					
Shop	2,568,796	2,886,288	3,006,550	3,267,989	3,985,352
Domestic	4,621,832	5,032,050	4,525,912	3,463,818	4,590,540
Overseas	49,082	88,193	186,611	451,386	135,640
Total	7,239,710	8,006,531	7,719,073	7,183,193	8,711,532
% to previous year Total		111%	96%	93%	121%
Net Income	590,036	196,160	185,258	61,057	583,673
Percentage to sales	8.15%	2.45%	2.40%	0.85%	6.70%
Advertising	4,871	7,338	6,869	8,805	8,013
R&D	9,453	10,281	3,798	2,234	18,485

Capital Expenditure	1,059,888	1,578,800	5,935,901	3,452,023	531,677
Long Term Debt	1,385,198	1,283,824	1,597,691	1,366,753	1,071,370
Total Assets	2,448,479	3,155,649	7,182,271	6,802,658	4,065,526

Source: Company Estimates

7

Web Reservations International[1]

JAMES A. CUNNINGHAM and WILLIE GOLDEN[2]

Never in our wildest dreams could we have expected this kind of growth, for two guys in Ireland to own a whole sector.

RAY NOLAN

The world of independent travelling using hostels offers great expectations, new life experiences and opportunities to make new friends. Independent travellers have to deal with balancing spontaneity with the desire to have certainty about travel and accommodation information. For the independent traveller hostels provide low-cost accommodation which are used as key staging bases for exploring new countries. Hostels, in addition to basic accommodation, can provide a range of services including bar, bike hire, common room, free airport pick up, guest kitchens, internal access, luggage storage and a travel information desk. Independent travellers exchange information about the best hostels to stay at, the tourist attractions to see and what fellow travelling partners to avoid on their travels. Colm Hanratty is one of these independent travellers but the difference is that he works for hostelworld.com who are global providers of online reservations to the budget, independent and youth travel market (BIYT), which is estimated to be worth $4.5 billion annually. Colm spent a year backpacking around Australia and has 'acquired a certain knack of hunting out bargains no matter how long it takes to sniff out, I will find them'. He regales readers on hostelworld.com with tales of where to go and what to see and where is the best nightlife and doing so on a low budget, for example a three-day trip to London for STG£119.36.

COMPANY BACKGROUND

Tom Kennedy owned the Avalon House Hostel in Dublin. In the mid 1990s, in an effort to make the business more efficient, he contracted Ray Nolan (an IT specialist, a self-taught computer programmer and owner of Raven Computing) to develop a software programme which would allow the hostel to manage the check-in and check-out process. After a successful installation of the software at Avalon House Hostel, Nolan resold the reservations management system as *backpack* to a number of hostels.

Table 7.1: **Management Team**

RAY NOLAN – CEO and founder

A seasoned entrepreneur and IT professional, Ray is CEO of Web Reservations International (WRI). He has been responsible for the growth strategy, using his experience in several facets of the software industry to implement business models that are both highly functional and profitable. Ray teams his market knowledge with core development skills to ensure projects deliver on their promise. Having successfully driven hostelworld.com to a dominant market position, Ray spends much of his time replicating the methodologies employed across the entire budget travel sector.

TOM KENNEDY – president and founder

Tom's years of industry experience are key to the success of the company. Accredited with helping the sector in Ireland move to a new level, his position as President allows him apply his knowledge on the world stage. With Ray, Tom realised that existing business processes could not be effectively applied to global distribution of budget product. A new model led to the birth of WRI. Tom spends his time strengthening relationships whilst continually refining the business model to create a win-win-win scenario for the company, the supplier and the consumer.

NIAMH NÍ MHIR – marketing director

WRI relies on three sources for customer acquisition: its own web presence, those of its partners and those of its suppliers. Niamh has created a marketing strategy that has made WRI sites the most popular in their sector. Meanwhile she ensures that partner sites get the product they need, delivered the way they want. Niamh keeps WRI alert to new opportunities in

---

a market that has evolved rapidly since the company first appeared in the budget sector.

FEARGAL MOONEY – COO

Companies experiencing the hyper growth experienced by WRI need to deliver on their promise. As Chief of Operations, Feargal ensures that correct procedures are in place and that the dreams of the entrepreneurs see profitable conclusion. His multinational finance experience additionally provides WRI with the metrics against which it constantly compares itself. The company can rely on sound financials, backed up by a comprehensive implementation team.

In 1999 Ray Nolan and Tom Kennedy founded Web Reservations International (WRI) and created an online reservation site for hostel bookings – www.hostelworld.com. The *backpack* software was modified to enable hostels to be seamlessly integrated with the online booking system at www.hostelworld.com. Ten copies of *backpack* were sold in 1999 and this figure had reached one hundred by 2001. They both decided to leave their respective jobs and WRI now employs 31 people. The company's revenue grew by 1,436 per cent from 2000 to 2002 compared to the industry average of 269 per cent for the top 50 technology companies in Ireland. The management team consists of Nolan as CEO, Kennedy as president, Niamh Ní Mhir as director of marketing and Feargal Mooney as COO (see Table 7.1). Nolan and Kennedy own 90 per cent of the business and the minority private investors are U2 manager Paul McGuinness and Paddy Holohan (entrepreneur and a former executive of Baltimore Technologies). WRI's multicultural staff work in a variety of roles including programming, content, sales and customer service, and all have experience of the budget travel industry from both business and pleasure perspectives. The combined travel experiences encompass over 75 countries. For customer relation staff positions, candidates must possess fluency in a number of languages, have previous experience in the hospitality industry and have good administration, telephone, keyboard and computer skills.

BIYT MARKET

According to industry forecasts the Budget, Independent and Youth Travel market (BIYT) will represent more than 25 per cent of all travel by 2005.

The BIYT market comprises of students, youths, backpackers and independent travellers. They are typically web-savvy, value conscious and tend to take extended vacations and set the travel trends for the business travellers of the future. Nolan (2002) describes this market '... as the most web-friendly segment of the market. Web Reservations International is already the leader in technology and booking revenue in this market and we intend to grow even faster in the future'.

Online travel companies, because of the low prices, low commission and margins, and the high cost of traditional booking systems, have neglected the BIYT sector. These traditional booking systems, called Global Distribution Systems (GDS), provide pre-internet travel booking systems. However, the high cost of installing and using GDS systems makes them unsuitable for both BIYT product providers and travel companies. In comparison, WRI's online booking system provides a web only, low-cost booking system, effectively becoming the GDS of the BIYT sector.

Traditionally, the value of the market was vastly underestimated as hostel bookings value ranged from €10 to €20 with a number of people sharing a room, but as Nolan highlights, 'It's one of the hidden facts about the tourist industry. Hostels are a very profitable business.' The entire market has changed, in many ways making the internet an obvious tool for reaching this market. No longer is the BIYT market consisting of poor students checking out the cheapest possible holidays. Nowadays, hostellers and budget travellers are often older people or families, with hostels now offering single and family rooms to cater to this market, in addition to multi-bed dormitories. Hostellers and backpackers carry credit cards and typically go online daily in internet cafes, making online booking a simple transaction. Moreover, they demand a more structured travel experience, seeking outdoor adventure or cultural activities and tours. WRI's online reservation system and websites cater for this demand. In addition, they spend plenty of money in restaurants rather than cooking in a communal hostel kitchen. Reflecting on these market changes, Kennedy notes that: 'A few years ago, a hostel would have been full of people cooking their pasta or lentils and they would all arrive by bike. Now everyone arrives by taxi from the ferry or airport and they all head into town for dinner.'

CREATING THE ELECTRONIC MARKETPLACE

The changes in the BIYT market, coupled with the successful redevelopment of the *backpack* software and the hostelworld.com website, afforded WRI a dominant position in this market. Both Nolan and

Kennedy, who ran Avalon House Hostel in Dublin, realised that while it was time-consuming and labour-intensive for an individual hostel to deal with e-mails and booking software – Kennedy had two people doing nothing but that – an automated booking service for hundreds or thousands of hostels could be the basis of a solid business. As Nolan states, 'Budget tourism was totally bypassed by technology until we came along … it was not serviced online before we existed. We created the industry'. In the early 1990s the 15,000 hostels worldwide generally ran their own individual websites, with no credit card booking facilities. Typically hostel users may spend less per night but go away for longer periods of time and therefore spend more money than average travellers. By 2003, WRI had built relationships with 5,000 hostels and was selling rooms on their behalf through an integrated internet reservation system.

THE BACKPACK SOFTWARE

The core product offered to individual hostels is *backpack* – a reservation management system for the youth hostels and budget accommodation. The software integrates fully with WRI websites. It allows hostel owners to upload and download bookings, browse for availability, search for guests, review pending arrivals and set room accommodation allocations. When a booking occurs the budget accommodation owner can view and print invoices, letters and vouchers and any field within the guest booking can be changed. The software generates several reports that assist in the management of the accommodation centre. These reports include the end of shift payment analysis, bookings by booking source, income analysis, stock analysis and credit card pre-authorisation.

WRI WEBSITE

WRI's main site www.hostelworld.com allows visitors to choose a destination or hostel, select an arrival date and the duration of their stay and then it quotes prices in whichever currency they wish to use, making the booking procedure extremely straightforward. Once a hostel has been selected, detailed information is provided on the hostel's location, photographs of the exterior and interior, currency converter, room reviews and all other relevant information for the chosen accommodation. As well as the booking facility, WRI provide guides to the various continents, countries and cities where hostels are located. City guides provide lists of pubs, clubs and attractions, with an interactive map to locate each one, and contain information on transport, weather, opening hours, public holidays, tourist offices, etc. In essence, WRI websites provide all the necessary information a traveller needs to know before booking accommodation.

WRI's best-known and flagship website www.hostelworld.com is aimed at the backpacker and student market and attracts over 12 million visitors annually. However, this is not the company's only site. It also operates and runs a number of hotel sites for city, country and continent sites, such as hosteldublin.com and hosteleurope.com. Another website is trav.com, which offers budget accommodation, tours, activities, transport, travel insurance and ancillary products for the BIYT market. Things2do.com, a recent addition to WRI, provides online booking and information for adventure activities, sightseeing tours, events and transport, as well as accommodation including hostels, budget hotels and guesthouses. Linked to the BIYT market focus, WRI runs www.insureandtravel.com that sells online insurance policies for backpackers and student travellers. WRI runs 500 websites targeted at the BIYT market (see Table 7.2). The online service confirms online reservations for budget accommodation and other complementary travel products.

Table 7.2: **Sample of WRI Websites**

Flagship Websites
www.hostelworld.com
www.trav.com
www.things2do.com
www.discounthotels-world.com
www.insureandtravel.com
www.hostels.com

The purpose of having 500 individual sites is to ensure that anybody searching for a hostel will ultimately land on a WRI site. The success of this strategy can be seen in the fact that sites controlled by WRI dominate any Google search for hostel accommodation in any major town or city in the world. This internet-based marketing strategy is consistent with the emphasis of being a low-cost operator. WRI uses search-engine optimisation and they present the same information in different formats depending on the website. So if an online user is looking for hostel accommodation in South Africa, a search engine might direct you to any one of sites that they own, namely: hosteljohannesburg.com, hostelsouthafrica.com or hostelafrica.com. In 2003, WRI generated more than 3 million bed/night bookings and attracted over 30 million visitors to its various websites. Of the WRI's revenue, 50 per cent is now generated from its own websites.

THE REVENUE MODEL

When using WRI's websites, travellers are told immediately if a hostel has space, which they can then book and reserve right away by having a 10 per cent deposit and a small booking fee charged to a credit card. WRI offers the rooms at the price the hostel charges, making its money by keeping the 10 per cent charge and the fee. The margins may be very small on a typical €10 hostel bed, but with 6,000 hostels in nearly 130 countries and 460 cities, WRI does very well on volume. WRI have not altered the revenue model for industry participants, but they have provided a dominant electronic market forum for this international market. As Nolan (2003) describes, 'When we sell a ticket, we are automatically out of the game and because we have hostels in both the southern and the northern hemispheres, we don't have a slow season'. This has resulted in profits increasing by 400 per cent in 2003 with forecasts for similar performances in the next four years. Central to this is WRI's ability to keep the cost base low and communications to a minimum. The business is entirely internet based and the premise is that if an employee has to lay a finger on a booking, WRI loses money. Given this premise and the increase in sales volume since 2000, the cost of making €1 revenue has fallen from €2.56 to 41 cent.

AFFILIATE SITES

In pursing its dominance of the BIT market, WRI licenses its reservation technology to a wide range of affiliate travel websites (Table 7.3). The number of affiliates using WRI's online booking technology reached 700 by 2004. WRI has targeted the travel agent market overlooked by many industry players in the dot.com rush. WRI have established a Travel Agent Extranet System for this market coupled with a loyalty card. This means that travel agents do not have to contract individual rates, but they have direct access to worldwide budget accommodation. As Kennedy (2003) states, 'We have developed the software to benefit travel agents and affiliates such as Rough Guide and Time Out, which can offer a worldwide reach to accommodation and share in the commission we can generate.'

Table 7.3: **Sample of WRI Affiliate Licences**

Affiliate Licenses
www.studentuniverse.com
www.lonelyplanet.com
www.ryanair.com
www.letsgo.com
www.raileurope.com
www.kasbah.com
www.ebookers.com

TOUR/ACTIVITY PROVIDERS

WRI's internet reservation system is now being used by customers to book not just their hostel room, but also other elements of their holiday. Such activities may include museum tickets, exhibitions, city tours, bungee jumping, rafting, abseiling, skydiving, etc. For example, Nolan (2003) states that, 'some 40 per cent of people booking a Dublin stay through a WRI site also book Aircoach tickets'. WRI takes an annual fee ($500 per year for one listing, $800 per year for two to four listings and $1,000 for 5+ tours) and 10 per cent reservation fee from tour operators for complementary products they sell through its websites.

COMPETITION

The principal competition comes from Expedia and Travelocity, who were ranked number one and two respectively by hitwise.com in terms of travel agency sites visited in the US in December 2003. Expedia had 22.82 per cent market share while Travelocity had 16.35 per cent (http://www.clickz.com/stats/markets/travel/article.php/6071_3304691). Expedia's gross bookings for the first quarter of 2004 were $2,672m, while Travelocity had sales of $394.5m in 2003. In comparison, WRI expects to sell more than €100 million worth of accommodation by the end of 2004.

MARKET EXPANSION AND GROWTH

Since the foundation of the business, Nolan and Kennedy were keen to become dominant players in the BIT market through organic growth and acquisitions. Hostels.com has been in operation since 1994 and had a well-established brand name in the market, listing over 6,000 hostels worldwide. Hostels.com received numerous industry awards (Yahoo Internet Life,

CNET EZ Connect) and had over 10 million page requests per month for a variety of services including hostel accommodation, rail and airline tickets, car hire and travel guidebooks.

In a bold strategic move WRI acquired hostels.com in January 2003. It was a key player in the BIYT market and was a good fit with WRI in relation to market and product fit. Commenting on the acquisition Nolan (2003) stated, 'We put our money where our mouth was because it was more cash than we had available to us. If anyone wanted to compete against us, the purchase of hostels.com set them back years.' Kennedy stated that:

> The purchase of hostels.com is an important strategic move for us – it gives us more hostel booking, more hostel product and an unrivalled brand name that is synonymous with our business of hostel reservations. In a single deal we have doubled our property base from which we can grow revenue streams even faster than previously.

Industry analysts estimated that this acquisition had the potential to treble WRI's turnover to €65 million and would see them out-booking their combined competitors by a ratio of ten to one.

Over a year later, WRI acquired Hostels of Europe, which provided marketing support and operated a website featuring 450 hostels throughout Europe. Ní Mhir (2004) commented that, 'The purchase of Hostels of Europe strengthens our position as the main distribution channel for hostel beds worldwide. Europe is our largest market for hostel booking and is a dynamic sector'.

INDUSTRY AWARDS

WRI kept a low profile until 2002 when it recorded its one millionth hostel bed night sale and, as Nolan put it, 'People started to notice the small Dublin company that was attracting more than two million visitors a month to its website ... like it or not, the limelight has started to find Nolan and Kennedy'. WRI has now won many industry accolades. The first award that catapulted hostelworld.com into the limelight was when it received the best e-commerce award and the overall EsatBT Award at the 2002 Golden Spiders Internet Awards ceremony. Being short-listed for the United National Industrial Development Organisation (UNIDO) followed; the judging panel praised the company for its combination of innovation, clarity, spectacular growth and its profitable business model. From more than 800 entries from over 136 countries, hostelworld.com was selected and named as one of 40 of the world's best content websites by the World Summit Award Grand Jury. Another accolade followed for hostelworld.com when it was short-listed for the Ernst and Young Entrepreneur of the Year Award 2003. The company won the Emerging Entrepreneur of the Year Award. In October 2003 the company was awarded second place at the Deloitte and Technology Fast 50 Awards ceremony. Reflecting on the award, Nolan said, 'This award reflects revenue growth, but here at WRI we have always focused, not just on growing revenues but on growing profits. From the outset WRI has been doing what dotcom companies originally set out to do – to utilise technology to rapidly grow their business.'

FUTURE CHALLENGES

Since the acquisition of hostels.com in January 2003 speculation has surrounded the future direction of WRI and whether Nolan and Kennedy would sell the business. In early 2004 WRI had received informal sounds from Summit Partners (www.summitpartners.com), a leading private equity and venture capital firm that has a capital base in excess of $5.5 billion. Summit has a proven track record of providing equity to high growth firms since its foundation in 1984 and has successfully managed over 100 public offerings and 80 strategic mergers or sales. Typically, its equity/debt investments span a variety of growing industries and range from $2 million to $250 million. Their tentative interest in WRI comes at a time when the company faced a number of significant challenges that would ultimately set the future direction of the company and its 31 employees. Travelling home to Clontarf on his Piaggio 180 scooter Nolan thought about whether the company should explore the Summit Partners tentative interest in WRI. WRI's strategy is further dominance and defence of its market position of the BIYT sector. Further organic growth and acquisitions outside hostel and budget accommodation were considered as the most likely strategic options to grow the business.

An earlier management meeting generated a lot of discussion about the future direction of the company. The main issue is how WRI would continue to maintain its dominant position in the BIYT market and transfer its technology and business model to the low-cost hotels market or some other sector of the travel industry. The issue of further investment in development of new products and further online functionality was also discussed at length. The issue of trust and security in relation to its 500 websites and affiliate programmes could become an issue in the future given the lack of an overall brand for WRI. Summit Partners valued WRI at about €100 million. The cost of making €1 of revenue had fallen from €2.56 in 1999 to 41 cent in 2003 and forecasted to drop by another 20 cent in the next few years.

The company had survived 9/11 and SARS and made significant acquisitions in hostel.com and Hostels of Europe without outside financial investment. Currently, with its technology and through targeting a disparate group of sellers, some 7,000 hostels in over 45 countries avail of its websites. In order to compete with peer competitors such as expedia.com from an Irish base Nolan realised the company would need to continue to expand rapidly to ensure its dominance strategy and to replicate its business model into other growing sectors of the travel industry. Approaching home, the question that kept nagging Nolan, given the challenges that WRI faces, was how best to pursue a dominant expansion strategy. Should the company pursue the venture capitalist route or continue to grow the business through internal financing?

NOTES
1. This case is intended to be used as the basis for class discussion rather than to illustrate either effective or ineffective handling of a management situation.
2. Dr James A. Cunningham is a College Lecturer in Strategic Management at the Department of Management, NUI, Galway and Dr Willie Golden is a Senior Lecturer in MIS within the Department of Accountancy and Finance at NUI, Galway.

CASE
HISTORIES

8

Abrakebabra[1]

ROSALIND BEERE and PETER MCNAMARA[2]

In 1982 two brothers, Wyn and Graeme Beere, founded what in twenty years' time would become Ireland's largest Irish owned fast food franchise. In the early 1980s Graeme was selling fast food at the front of an off-licence (Deveney's) in the Rathmines area of central Dublin. Wyn was working as a Chartered Surveyor in a prestigious international property firm. Dublin lacked the restaurant culture of other European cities. Instead, Dublin's social life centred on its vibrant pub culture, with bars focusing on drink sales rather than offering any variety of food to customers. All pubs closed simultaneously at 11p.m. nightly. Graeme noticed an important gap in the market – where do people go for food after a night out? The entrepreneurial solution was to create a fast food restaurant that specifically catered for this market. The offering would be new for Dublin: a product mix of kebabs, burgers and chips, popular in London at the time, and late opening until 4a.m. Searching for a name for this venture Graeme chose a play on words: a mix of the name of a Steve Miller number one record in 1982 'Abracadabra' and the kebab as the central product. In 1982 the newly named 'Abrakebabra' opened, a 'licence to print money', as one of the founders put it. The two brothers went from one owner-operated, small fast food restaurant in 1982 to a peak of 59 franchised outlets in the late 1990s. Through entrepreneurial leadership they survived two recessions and a franchisee revolt. This partnership was unbroken until 2001 when one of the brothers (Wyn) decided to retire from the business. His 50 per cent stake was bought out by Gaiety Investments Ltd, the venture capital vehicle of leading Irish entrepreneur, Denis Desmond. The exit of Wyn and the entry of Gaiety Investments Ltd presented both a challenge and an opportunity to the company. The challenge was how to move from an entrepreneurial mode of control to a more formal managerial control system. The opportunity was that a fresh equity injection by Denis Desmond could help fuel the expansionary strategy of Abrakebabra.

THE FRANCHISE REVOLT[3]

By 1997, Abrakebabra ran eleven company-owned restaurants. These restaurants had delivered powerful advantages to the brothers in the past. They had been an important source of cash flow during the development of the business-franchising model. Company-owned restaurants were also an important learning mechanism. By 1997, however, these company-owned units were consuming the majority of the brothers' management time. Resources spent on these restaurants meant less managerial attention could be given to the running of their franchising system, which at that time represented over 80 per cent of the company's restaurants.

A decision needed to be made about the long-term strategy of the firm as to whether it could continue to function effectively with such a split focus, between being a franchiser and a restaurateur. In response to the strategy crisis, the decision was made to franchise out all company-owned restaurants. Graeme Beere recently summarised the strategic logic of moving to a franchise-only management system as follows:

> The success of Abrakebabra is all about location, location, location. It is a hands-on cash business and we don't want investors, we want owner-occupiers … We found the key was to franchise out the outlets and concentrate on the brand … The wake-up came when our accountant told us that 80 per cent of our income came from franchising, but that 80 per cent of our time was spent on the 11 stores. We put franchisees into all of our stores and turnover increased immediately. All our head office time is now spent looking after the brand and franchisees who need help.[4]

However, trouble was on the horizon in the form of a group of franchisees who expressed concerns over the management of the Abrakebabra franchising network. Some of them claimed they were unhappy with the lack of management focus. It became apparent that a number of franchisees were arranging secret meetings to which the Abrakebabra management team were not invited. The brothers decided to confront this possible revolt head on. They called individual meetings with the franchisees. During these meetings the benefits of being an Abrakebabra franchisee were clearly communicated. Any franchisee that was not clearly committed to the Abrakebabra ethos was then released from their contract.

The experience of the franchisee revolt highlighted issues faced by the partners and their control mechanisms. The Abrakebabra management team created a new identity centred on an exclusively franchise-driven business growth model. This case explores the extent of goal alignment between the franchisees and the franchiser and the management control systems that the brothers installed to maximise value creation for both parties.

PERFORMANCE OF ABRAKEBABRA

By 2003 Abrakebabra's new managerial control system had yielded considerable dividends. Abrakebabra had maintained its position as the largest Irish-owned franchise network in its business domain – with 55 franchises. Only McDonald's was larger, with 66 franchise outlets (see Table 8.1 for size of main competitors). This success had also facilitated the exit of one of the founding brothers (Wyn) and a fresh injection of capital with the entry of Gaiety Investments as a major shareholder. Gaiety Investment's 50 per cent stake cost a reported €3.8 million, valuing Abrakebabra at €7.6 million by the end of 2002.[5]

Table 8.1: **Main Franchise Restaurant Outlets Operating Ireland in 2003**[6]

Name	Seating Availability	Number of Restaurants	Ownership
Abrakebabra	Seating	55	Irish
Supermacs	Seating	45	Irish
McDonald's	Seating	66	U.S.
Burger King	Seating	22	U.K.
Four Star Pizza	No Seating	26	U.S.
Domino's Pizza	No Seating	17	U.S.

In 2003, Abrakebabra had sales of €33 million, with the typical franchisee restaurant generating individual sales of €300,000 to €380,000. Franchisees pay a fee of 6 per cent on gross sales, after Value Added Tax, with a further 1 per cent advertising levy. The set-up costs for a franchisee are estimated to be €50,000 (all financial figures from www. abrakebabra.net). These charges grant franchisees use of the Abrakebabra brand name, purchasing systems and franchisee supports, as outlined below. Profit margins for franchisees are estimated to be as high as 20 per cent.[7] The *Sunday Business Post* indicated that expected profits for the year ended December 2002 were €1.1 million[8] for the Abrakebabra group, whilst actual profits were later reported to be over €900,000, up 350 per cent on 2001 profits.[9]

The exact profitability of both the franchising network and individual franchisees are difficult for external third parties to confirm independently. This is because the size of Abrakebabra means that full profit and loss accounts do not need to be made publicly available by the Irish Companies Registration Office (CRO). An analysis of the abridged accounts (primarily balance sheet information) that are publicly available from the CRO is complicated by changes in the structure of the organisation. Over the last ten years Abrakebabra operations have encompassed a number of companies including Abrakebabra Holdings, Abrakebabra Limited, Abrakebabra Franchising and Abrakebabra Meats, amongst others. An analysis of the abridged accounts of these firms does not offer significant insights into the underlying profitability of the franchiser.[10] These firms are not required to publish sales figures through the CRO, thus external parties cannot observe the amount of levies raised from franchisees.

What lies behind the valuation of Abrakebabra itself and the profits generated by individual franchisees is the franchise-led growth strategy and managerial control systems installed in the wake of the 1997 franchisee revolt. From 1997, emphasis was placed on running Abrakebabra as a core franchising support system. With no company-owned restaurants to manage, the two brothers were able to formulate a new strategy that focused exclusively on a franchising business model. A number of unsuitable franchisees did not adhere to the Abrakebabra ethos and exited the franchising system. The process of franchising out company-owned restaurants, the experience of the franchisee revolt and exit of unsuitable franchisees, led management to a realisation that the quality of their franchisees was just as important as the total number of franchisees in the network. Thus, management looked at the franchising system with a new perspective.

THE FRANCHISER

The Abrakebabra management team, having franchised out the remaining company-owned restaurants, began to reassess their role as a franchiser. In the aftermath of the franchisee revolt the management sought clarification of the value Abrakebabra Ltd created for its franchisees, both in its role as the strategic centre and as operational services provider. At this time Abrakebabra decided to reconsider their key objectives as a franchiser. The financial accountant, Dominic Kelly, noted that:

> Your average Managing Director's role in life is to increase his shareholders wealth. Ultimately that means getting rich. Shareholder value is created in two ways … You either create profits which generate dividends or you create a business that is worth money even if it's not necessarily paying dividends.[11]

The firm sought to maximise long-term shareholder value through a twin focus on profit maximisation and sustainable growth of its franchising network. These goals were achieved by delivering and capturing value for the franchisees. Abrakebabra now saw their core competencies as being divided into four domains: the first domain was brand identity; the second was new product development; the third was centralised purchasing to attain economies of scale; and the fourth was training, mentoring and franchisee management. Additionally the franchiser would provide support services to the franchisees such as legal services, capital acquisition and property management advice. Do franchisees believe that these benefits accrue from membership of the Abrakebabra franchisee network? Seven franchisees' perspectives on why they are members of Abrakebabra are provided in Appendix 8.1. This evidence indicates that in general franchisees concur with management on the benefits of being a franchisee of Abrakebabra.

The management team could see the obvious benefits of franchising as a system of growth and they redefined and reasserted the advantages of such a structure. The company had achieved rapid expansion and market penetration with relatively low capital investment. Abrakebabra had been able to expand the number of outlets, increase market coverage, market share and brand equity with limited financial exposure. In addition, individual restaurant operational duties were delegated to franchisees and profits increased through the enhanced motivation of these individual operators. Attributed to the fact that individual franchisees have made significant financial investments in their business and are thus more likely to be motivated to maximise sales and minimise costs, when compared with hired managers in the same position. Furthermore, Abrakebabra also benefits from a positive cash flow and risk is transferred away from the company because the franchisees accept all financial, human resource and business risk themselves, limiting the financial liability of Abrakebabra should an individual franchise fail.

However, after identifying the positives, to achieve their new focus, the Abrakebabra team set about looking at the disadvantages of franchising and the potential problem areas needing to be addressed. Key problems were the control and monitoring of the franchisees' performance in terms of financial performance and restaurant standards. The management team acknowledged the difficulty in exercising tight controls over the franchisees, due to the nature of the relationship as stipulated in the franchise agreement. Indeed a crucial problem faced by the management team is to ensure that franchisees declare their true level of business activity. Another challenge is to verify that franchisees are achieving and maintaining the highest standards in their restaurants. The Abrakebabra management team knew that they needed to readdress these key areas. In doing this they also needed to define their franchisees' objectives and try to align further both parties' goals and priorities.

THE FRANCHISEE

An important goal of a franchisee is the maximisation of wealth. How can Abrakebabra help maximise wealth? What benefits should the franchisees be receiving from Abrakebabra? The Abrakebabra website points to three benefits of becoming a franchise: it is easier to raise finance, the risk of failure is lower and franchisees can use a product of proven appeal (www.abrakebabra.net). The management team recognised that Abrakebabra's proven track record and success with earlier franchisees had provided new franchisees with a tried and tested business formula. Abrakebabra thereby link the financial goals of the franchisee with the success of the franchiser. Other benefits experienced by the franchisee are as follows: access to Abrakebabra's investment in new product development and large marketing programmes; the opportunity to be their own boss, while having access to the Abrakebabra experience through supervision and consultation; and economies of scale in purchasing, advertising, staff training and reduced operating costs. These advantages lie beyond the reach of a sole trader, but are available to a franchisee.

Possible shortcomings of Abrakebabra as a franchiser also needed to be considered by the management team. Franchisees may find the restrictions of the non-negotiable franchise agreement unattractive. Abrakebabra may not live up to a franchisee's expectations. Brand mismanagement by Abrakebabra might harm the whole system. The franchisee may not be able to avail of new supply opportunities because they are locked into buying from a designated supplier of Abrakebabra. The management team needed to ensure that such problem issues would be avoided.

THE CONTRACT: THE FRANCHISE AGREEMENT

In looking at the relationship between Abrakebabra and its franchisees, the management team needed to assess the most critical document governing this relationship: the franchise agreement. This defined each party's legally binding obligations, duties and rights. Abrakebabra writes the contract and the terms are non-negotiable because the company is the owner of the brand and its associated trademarks. The agreement grants the franchisee exclusive rights to operate an Abrakebabra restaurant at an approved location and to use Abrakebabra's trademarks and other rights of the company in conjunction with the operation of the restaurant. The rights and responsibilities associated with an Abrakebabra franchise agreement require that all franchisees pay an initial fee for a single restaurant, a 6 per cent franchise royalty fee and 1 per cent for group advertising. In order to calculate this figure, franchisees are required to submit to the company weekly sales reports for their respective restaurant.

In return for the initial fee and royalty payments, Abrakebabra helps to set up a franchisee's restaurant, together with the provision of training and general assistance in central services such as: brand awareness, bulk buying, health and safety training and standards maintenance. The Abrakebabra management also lend their expertise in property selection and the fitting out of a new restaurant. In addition franchisees receive continuous supervisory support from Head Office and have an assigned area supervisor who carries out regular visits. A quarterly newsletter is also produced at Head Office and distributed to all franchisees, describing operational changes, current food prices, management advice and assistance. If a franchisee has any issues they contact Head Office or their area supervisor via telephone and assistance is immediate.

After assessing the key issues, the management team considered that the contract was not the central concern that needed to be addressed. In their view the key problems were those that could arise after the contract was signed, such as the ongoing monitoring of operational and financial performance of a franchisee. Careful selection of franchisees could assist in minimising both performance problems and the risk of a future franchisee revolt.

FRANCHISEE SELECTION

Abrakebabra realised that the success of their franchising system was highly dependent upon the quality of their franchisees and so an important issue facing them was how to ascertain a potential franchisee's level of quality. The problems that Abrakebabra faced in selecting a new franchisee was that potential candidates could appear to be suitable at first glance but over time could be deemed unsuitable.

Originally, franchisees had been chosen on the basis that they had the financial resources and background necessary to run a successful franchise restaurant. Abrakebabra's management quickly made themselves acquainted with the background of franchising laws and issues. As a result of the success experienced by the company during 1982–1990, Abrakebabra was inundated with interested candidates. Consequently Abrakebabra was able to be more selective in choosing its franchisees. However, the recruitment process had remained relatively informal.

After the franchisee revolt the management team decided to make the process more formal. They set about formulating a selection system to help identify suitable franchisees. The process is as follows: first, all potential franchisees have to fill out a formal application form, providing basic personal details and the amount of capital available for investment. If chosen, they will be interviewed in a first round of interviews by David Zebedee, the franchise director. He evaluates each franchisee's ambitions, intentions and personal characteristics. Abrakebabra also look for commitment to the company, because each new franchisee signs a ten-year contract. They do not want investors who only give monetary investments and fail to run the restaurant properly. The type of franchisees that Abrakebabra want is someone with experience in management and entrepreneurship. They want people with ambition and passion to run a restaurant full time, serving customers to the best of their ability. They want people with ideas and drive and with a strong sense of responsibility to the franchiser, their customers and community. Previous education is not as important as previous experience in business, especially in the food business, or any business dealing with customers and staff. Franchisees vary from those who have completed primary education through to university graduates. They generally find that the best franchisees have a good combination of experience and education.

TRAINING OF A FRANCHISEE

When a franchisee is selected and deemed suitable to run and operate an

Abrakebabra franchise, official training begins. The company has found that over the years the best possible form of training is on-the-job with another franchisee. A new recruit is assigned to an established franchisee and works up through the ranks in a restaurant until they are capable of operating and managing it. This form of training can take from two weeks to three months. The trainee must have a thorough knowledge of the restaurant and all its internal procedures and activities. The franchisee must be competent in all tasks needed to run a successful Abrakebabra franchise restaurant, such as cooking techniques, till operation, financial management and reporting, supplier management, stock control, health and safety requirements, human resource management and customer management, amongst other skills and competencies. Once selected and trained as a franchisee, they enter a long-term ten-year contract with Abrakebabra.

MANAGING THE RELATIONSHIP BETWEEN THE FRANCHISEE AND FRANCHISER

Abrakebabra the franchiser, makes its profits from each individual franchisee's entry fee (lump sum) and an ongoing 6 per cent levy on all franchisee's gross revenues (excluding the 1 per cent advertising levy). For this fee, Abrakebabra needs to ensure that all franchisees deliver consistent product and service quality levels to the end customer. In return, Abrakebabra provides good support infrastructure for their franchisees. Franchisees make their profit by efficient management of operations and the attraction of customers into their restaurant in preference to rival operations. Dominic Kelly states:

> If you consider that your food is costing you say 35 per cent for an average week … your wages are costing you 25 per cent, that's 60 per cent of your turnover gone. Now out of that you've got 40 per cent left to pay all the rest of your overhead, including financing costs, so really you can see where all of a sudden that 5 per cent of your gross profit becomes critical because the difference between having 40 per cent or 45 per cent left, that might be the difference between make or break. With the franchising system profits are maximised.[12]

Franchisees pay the franchiser for their expertise in operational issues, access to economies of scale, supply chain management, bulk buying, marketing and branding. All of these benefits make the franchisee more cost efficient than if they acted as a sole trader. One example of the benefits that access to bulk purchasing is the supply deal with C&C for soft drinks. In return for exclusive supply of soft drinks C&C (distributors of Pepsi and Club orange) contributes about half of the total marketing budget of Abrakebabra.[13] This enables the network to keep the advertising levy at 1 per cent of franchisee sales. Abrakebabra's management have suggest that 'bulk buying offers Abrakebabra operators an extra 10 per cent profit margin over and above the industry norm of 60 percent'.[14]

Broadly speaking the franchisees appear to concur with Abrakebabra's perspective on the royalty fee. However, Abrakebabra needs to ensure that franchisees maximise their gross revenue and maintain high levels of product and service quality. Maximisation of revenues means increased profit for Abrakebabra through the franchisee royalty fee levied on each franchisee's operation. Maintenance of high levels of product and service quality ensures that Abrakebabra will be successful as a franchising system in both end-consumer markets and in the attraction of future franchisees. Thus, Abrakebabra needs to ensure that franchisees are consistent in the following: use of the brand, restaurant design and maintenance, health and safety, product quality and customer service. Franchisees face a difficulty in that maintenance of these standards may suppress their profits. The central question is how Abrakebabra can ensure that on the one hand, these standards (costs) are maintained equally by all franchisees and on the other hand, franchisees accurately report weekly gross revenues to head office (thus attracting a total 7 per cent levy; 6 per cent for royalty fee and 1 per cent for advertising budget). Over the years Abrakebabra have installed and modernised a series of monitoring and control systems to manage these two key issues. The challenge faced by Abrakebabra is the large cost involved in monitoring these standards, all of which must be absorbed from the revenues that they derive from the 6 per cent levy on franchisee's revenues (excluding the 1 per cent advertising levy). In relation to franchising, the quality of service at individual outlets needs to be consistent and must meet a pre-ordained minimum standard. The franchisee's quality of effort and meeting of contractual requirements needs to be continuously monitored.

The Abrakebabra management team looked at a number of contractual clauses in the franchise agreement, which stipulated how the franchisees should operate their outlets. The clauses specify and regulate how the business should be run on a daily basis and shape its long-term development. These control systems fall into two categories: monitoring of operational tasks and attainment of strategic goals. The first category is designed to regulate day-to-day business and these include hours of operation, prices, product quality, accounting systems, layout, décor and Abrakebabra's right to inspect the premises and make changes unilaterally. These contractual clauses allow the company to control their franchisees' daily operations and ensure that the franchisees uniformly follow the 'ideal' business format model. The second category involves more strategic controls that shape the longer-term business trajectory. This group of controls include sales targets and objectives, expansion triggers, contract duration, contract renewal and a contract termination option. Abrakebabra creates operational controls to establish, maintain and increase the business's turnover (upon which they received percentage fees), whereas franchisees are more interested in maximising profit.

The Abrakebabra management team then turned to how they physically monitor franchisees. The first of these methods is through financial monitoring. Every Monday, franchisees must call in their previous week's sales figures to head office. These figures are then checked off against previous years, with profit and loss assessments being checked and maintained over time. To improve both the accuracy and efficiency of monitoring revenues the franchiser's management team have begun to install modems in every Abrakebabra franchisee till. This means that all sales information from a till is immediately relayed to head office, ensuring that Abrakebabra maintains direct contact with a franchisee's sales status. The modems not only allow the management to monitor sales figures but also give vital information on the success of their product mix and whether certain products are increasing in popularity. If on the other hand certain products are under-performing, promotional campaigns can be targeted at these products. In addition, the sales information helps the company monitor year-on-year sales progress. This use of technology is an important monitoring asset for the management team. The benefits of this new system would at first appear to be weighted in favour of the franchiser. However, the weekly chore that every franchisee faces on a Friday and a Monday of calculating their weekly turnover and relaying this information to head office will be eliminated, thus benefiting them in saving time and effort.

The second and equally important method of monitoring for the Abrakebabra management team is the use of standards. Abrakebabra has a team who are divided into four areas in Ireland: north, south, east and west. Regional team supervisors visit their respective franchisees on a systematic and regular basis. Somebody will visit each franchisee at least twice a month from head office to check standards. A hygiene audit is done at least every six weeks in every store. In addition to this, Abrakebabra has a health and safety officer who also must check and maintain records of each restaurant's standard. All of the above monitoring checks are recorded in report form and delivered to head office. Any problems are dealt with immediately.

Customers are also a great source of monitoring. Customer comment cards are available in all restaurants. Customers can (and do) phone Abrakebabra headquarters directly if they wish to make a complaint about service provision in an individual franchise restaurant. The information received from this form of direct consumer response monitoring is essential for the management team.

Finally, mystery shoppers are also employed by the Abrakebabra management. The feedback received from this method of monitoring is a great way of surveying franchisees' standards and competence levels.

CONCLUSION

From a franchisee's perspective it is clear that the changes in strategy post 1997 have delivered increased value for them. As one franchisee put it:

> I'd say that the brand has really improved in the last couple of years … I think they have taken a far more professional approach – to the business … You know, when I was setting up they did everything they could for me.[15]

From the perspective of the franchiser the changes post 1997 have also been successful. From a difficult position in 1997, with franchisees in open revolt, the management have turned the firm around. Franchisees now see the value that the franchiser creates. New franchisees are being attracted to the venture and opportunities to attract fresh capital have arisen. The question for the management team at Abrakebabra now is how far and how long can the growth model be sustained?

NOTES
1. This case is intended to be used as the basis for class discussion rather than to illustrate either effective or ineffective handling of a management situation.
2. Rosalind Beere is a Research Scholar at Trinity College Dublin and Peter McNamara is a Lecturer in Strategy at University College Dublin.
3. A similar version of this case is available through the European Case Clearing House.
4. S. McMahon (2003) 'Franchising for the Future', *Sunday Business Post*, 25 May 2003.

5. *Business and Finance*, 'Desmond Invest €3.8 million in Abrakebabra', 11 April 2002.
6. All competitor information was obtained by contact with each company's head office.
7. B. O'Halloran (2002) 'Abrakebabra to Take a Bigger Bite of Fast Food Market', *Business and Finance,* 11 April 2002.
8. McMahon, op cit.
9. Business News (2004) 'Abrakebabra Works its Magic', *Sunday Business Post*, 22 February 2004.
10. As part of this case study the authors undertook an analysis of the abridged accounts of Abrakebabra Holdings and Abrakebabra Ltd using the published accounts from the CRO (www.cro.ie) in February 2004. Abrakebabra Franchising and Abrakebabra Meats were not in operation in 2004.
11. Interview with Dominic Kelly, Company Financial Accountant.
12. Ibid.
13. O'Halloran, op cit.
14. McMahon, op cit.
15. Interview with an Abrakebabra Franchisee.

Appendix 8.1: **The Franchisee's Perspective of Abrakebabra Membership**

Franchisee 1: 'Why Abra? Well at the time I looked at others. McDonald's, Supermacs, Abrakebabra, the whole package you know. I'd met every one of them and I'd just found them [Abrakebabra] to be the most attractive package out of the whole lot.'

'We [franchisees] are part of a big, bigger picture [in terms of] marketing and branding … more than independent outlets. And also from a financial point of view we are better off because we are purchasing at least 12–13 per cent cheaper than the small independent body would be doing.'

Franchisee 2: 'Why did I decide to franchise? Two reasons. I saw a strong name, with a strong product in a strong location and I went for it. Why did I decide to go Abra? Very strong and powerful product range, innovative [and] different.'

Franchisee 3: 'I was already in the business … and I knew that somebody would open up in [my area] if I didn't … so I got in there first! Why Abra? Because it was … how would you say … size basically. They had a presence … and [their design specifications] fitted the site … It wasn't big enough for McDonald's.'

Franchisee 4: 'We owned our own restaurant and McDonald's came to town. It [Abrakebabra] was something to do battle with McDonald's because it affected our business up to about a third of our trade dropped … because of that … I looked around at other franchises … I remember that I ate in Abrakebabra before and loved the food and so I made inquiries [about becoming a franchisee] and as a consequence we went for it.'

'Yes advertising and bulk buying would be the two main benefits … their back-up services are pretty good as well …'

Franchisee 5: 'I had looked around and McDonald's and Burger King had come to [my area] and I had seen Abra [as well]. I thought it would be good. I had gone along to a show in O'Reilly Hall in UCD and there was an Abra stand, a Pizza Hut stand … I went away and I didn't really know what to do. Then a while later I saw an ad in the paper and made the call to Abra and went from there.'

'Advertising and bulk buying, yes … they would be the biggest benefit … and of course they [Abrakebabra] help to solve problems with suppliers if a delivery hasn't been made or other stuff. Oh and the name is the biggest benefit of course.'

Franchisee 6: 'Advertising and bulk buying …'

Franchisee 7: 'Advertising, bulk buying and legal [expertise] … Wyn has a huge amount of experience in relation to landlords, dealing with veracious neighbours, rights of way, all this sort of thing. So that's always been a big, big help, they have a huge expertise which they accumulate …'

9
Aer Lingus[1]

DENIS G. HARRINGTON, THOMAS C. LAWTON
and TAZEEB S. RAJWANI[2]

When Willie Walsh took the helm at Ireland's national airline, Aer Lingus, he was under no illusion as to the scale of the challenge he faced. No one associated a spirit of enterprise with long-established state-owned companies. Change management, difficult in the most adaptive organisations, tends to be far more arduous in companies that have government as the sole shareholder. The twin themes of cost reduction and profit maximisation – core principles for private enterprise – have traditionally been only loosely adhered to by state-owned enterprises. As a consequence, management procedures can often be lethargic, if not apathetic and work practices are inflexible and closely monitored by powerful trade unions. Walsh, a 22-year veteran of Aer Lingus when he was appointed Chief Executive in October 2001, was no stranger to the internal challenges he faced. Externally, the challenges to the business were increasing at a tremendous pace. A cloud was gathering over the entire industry that would render a sense of urgency to his task that no previous CEO had faced. Global terrorism, transnational infectious diseases and, above all, the competitive threat posed by low fare airlines (LFAs) had taken a tremendous toll on the revenues and market share of national airlines. Aer Lingus posted an operating loss for 2001 of €50.4 million (US$49.5 million), compared with a profit of €79.0 million (US$78.5 million) in 2000.[3] It was clear to Walsh that nothing short of a strategic overhaul was needed, resulting in tough measures that had to be taken to revive the company. But how would Aer Lingus compete in a changed environment? How could the momentum for change and renewal be sustained? How could an entrepreneurial leadership style be influential? At stake was the very survival of Aer Lingus.

TAKING TO THE SKIES

Aer Lingus, the Gaelic Irish term for 'Air Fleet', operated its first flight on 27 May 1936. The aircraft was a de Havilland Dragon. It took off from Baldonnel Airport in south county Dublin destined for Bristol, England, with a full load of five passengers. In 1940, the company moved to its present location at Dublin Airport, just north of the capital. Following World War Two, Aer Lingus embarked on a major expansion of its British and European networks. By the early 1950s, it had spread its wings into Europe with services to Paris, Amsterdam and Lourdes.[4] Even though Shannon Airport was opened on the west coast in 1946, it was not until the late 1950s that Aer Lingus turned its attention to transatlantic destinations. In 1958, Aer Lingus inaugurated its first transatlantic services to New York and Boston. Over the next two and a half decades, Aer Lingus continued to develop its routes and schedules to Britain, the United States and mainland Europe.

The Oil Crises of 1973 and 1979 caused severe disruption to the aviation industry. Aer Lingus, like most other companies, began a program of diversification. New areas of business included maintenance services and managerial training for other airlines. In an attempt to stabilise profits from a seasonal tourist trade, they entered the hotel business. In addition, they formed an alliance with the banking firm Guinness Peat, creating a new company called Guinness Peat Aviation.[5]

In 1984, Aer Lingus Commuter was established to serve the UK markets. Two years later in 1986, Aer Lingus celebrated its fiftieth year in existence. A Dragon plane was taken on tour around Ireland to celebrate the occasion. The good times continued for Aer Lingus between 1987 and 1989, with new Boeing 737s arriving to replace the older ones and Fokker F-50s being added to the Commuter fleet. However, by the 1990s, after the passage of the deregulation act for the airline industry in Ireland, Aer Lingus faced serious difficulties, caused in part by the collapse of GPA. As a result, Aer Lingus had to reconsider several aspects of operation and operational policies, but it still found it difficult to produce a profit. In essence, Aer Lingus became a loss-making enterprise, kept afloat by government exchequer money. Consequently, in 1993 the Cahill Plan – 'strategy for the Future' – was introduced, with its principal focus being to return the core business of airline transportation to profitability.

On 1 June 2000, Aer Lingus became a full member of the oneworld alliance. This is a network of international airlines working to bring greater benefits to its customers and increased efficiencies to its members. Together with the oneworld partners – American Airlines, British Airways, Cathay Pacific, Finnair, Iberia, LanChile and Qantas – Aer Lingus became a global team player. Following the terrorist attacks on New York and Washington in 2001, Aer Lingus announced plans to layoff 40 per cent of its workforce. The company's new CEO, Willie Walsh, implemented a plan to ensure the future survival of Aer Lingus. A number of internal and external factors had already begun to whittle away the company profits. These included industrial relation disputes, the impact of the foot-and-mouth outbreak and the bad press surrounding CEO Michael Foley – in addition to the deepening global economic downturn. However, while the airline had problems before September 11th, these problems quickly became a crisis following the terrorist attacks. Today, Aer Lingus continues to operate its intra-European services from its main hub at Dublin and the company bases its North American fleet at Shannon on the west coast.

THE CHANGING MARKET

Today's highly competitive air travel industry is unrecognisable from its early days when dominated by state-owned flag carriers. The market for short-haul flights has changed rapidly and the low-cost airlines have gained a huge market share from the traditional flag carriers. Although certainly in the same industry, some might argue that traditional flag carriers such as BA and low-cost airlines such as Ryanair operate in different markets, the former competing in the quality sensitive market and the latter competing in the low price market. But belonging to different markets does not mean that firms cannot compete across markets. Indeed, airline competition in Europe has started changing ever more so after the terrorist attacks in the US.

Financial history reveals that the airline business has all the characteristics of 'binge/purge cycles'. In good times, companies accumulate enormous debts and buy planes in anticipation of continued growth. In bad times, airlines appeal for anti-trust relief to protect their monopoly at hub airports, while the state-owned carriers in Europe appeal for state aid. Even during good times the business can be very difficult. For example, in the extraordinarily prosperous late 1990s, airlines continued to make very ordinary return on capital. According to *Fortune* magazine, in the period 1995–2000, despite making total earnings of $23 billion, US airlines only managed to generate an 8 per cent return on capital.[6] This demonstrates the challenges involved in leading a major airline and attempting to create an environment in which change can be initiated and sustained.

REDEFINING MISSION AND DIRECTION AT AER LINGUS

The chief executive's statement in the 2001 Annual Report is indicative of Aer Lingus' long-term goals and objectives. In it, Willie Walsh states that:

> Conceptually, this is a simple business. In the past many airlines, Aer Lingus included, have been guilty of over complicating it. Aer Lingus is changing this strategy.[7]

The group had effectively redefined its mission statement, asserting the need to achieve sustained profitability through commercially viable products and practices involving a keen customer focus. The new strategic direction that Aer Lingus adopted was one of catering for all sides of the aviation market. Essentially, they were competing with the Ryanair model, in an attempt to capture increased market share in a growing segment, while still providing the service for which they are renowned. Aer Lingus was beginning to realise that there were consumers who did not need a sandwich, a drink or an internet connection on board; they just wanted to get to their destination safely and cheaply. Aer Lingus was always a 'customer-focused' company, but was now finally becoming more market focused. With the entrance of new competitors like Ryanair and easyJet, competition had increased, resulting in a noticeable difference in price. Aer Lingus was now committed to getting their customers to their destinations as cheaply, simply and efficiently as possible. Aer Lingus' strategy was a twin track one; namely to offer cheaper fares while maintaining its reputation as a 'full service' airline, where appropriate. In tandem with this, the company aimed to continue to drive down costs and introduce more cheap fares. It was no longer locked into the traditional ways of doing things and had taken the view that it is more important to fly to destinations where the consumer wants to go.

Some have argued that this strategic re-positioning was in response to a number of internal and external factors that had whittled away company profits. These included industrial relation disputes, the impact of the foot-and-mouth outbreak and the bad press surrounding CEO Michael Foley – in addition to the deepening global economic downturn. These variables necessitated a sharper examination of company direction and strategy implementation. As some commentators remarked, Aer Lingus could not cope with sharp falls in revenue; they are capital intensive and needed to maintain a network, which means high fixed costs. Aircraft cost up to €200 million each and an airline must fill as much as three quarters of its seats to make any profit. Indeed many analysts predict that within a few years, Europe will have as few as three international long haul airlines. Also, aviation is a highly political business – particularly in a region where governments often own large amounts of shares in their national carriers. Issues of national pride and employment have long outweighed financial logic and may continue to do so. Historically, carriers that have failed were propped up with state money. The result has been a plague of overcapacity and weak profit margins. Weak carriers hence have not left the industry but instead have been recapitalised.

CHANGING CEO, CHANGING FORTUNES

Two factors seem to bedevil the airline industry both in Europe and the US: huge loans and poor industrial relations. Modest rises in the interest burden relative to sales can affect the bottom line adversely and because margins are low, strikes – even short ones – can mean the difference between a profitable and a loss-making year. As a result, leaders nowadays need to have qualities that allow them to compete on the edge. They need to be closer to their workers and be different. Equally, they need to have an entrepreneurial mindset, with high energy, motivational skills, a vision for opportunity and a willingness to take risks to succeed.

Willie Walsh's predecessor, Michael Foley, had a marketing background, having worked as the president and chief executive of Heineken USA and chief executive of Heineken's Irish brewing unit, Murphy Brewery Ltd. When in 2001 Michael Foley became embroiled in two alleged cases of sexual harassment involving work colleagues, subsequently confirmed by an internal inquiry, he exited the company and a new chief executive was urgently needed to revive the fortunes of Aer Lingus. This individual was found in the person of Willie Walsh, who first joined Aer Lingus in 1979 as a cadet pilot. He climbed rapidly through the ranks at Aer Lingus to become, in 1998, chief executive of Futura, the group's Spanish charter subsidiary based in Palma. The company was crisis-ridden and had almost torn itself apart in inter-union strife. In many ways it was the perfect training ground for what would await him at Aer Lingus. He admitted that his time in Spain, running what was a highly autonomous unit, might have allowed him to appreciate the big picture, which assisted his overall perception of opportunity when he eventually arrived back in Dublin during the summer of 2000 to become chief operations officer (COO). In the autumn of 2001, with both the departure of the existing CEO, Michael

Foley, and the tragic events of September 11th sending the airline reeling, Walsh was in the right place at the right time.[8] He was far removed from the traditionally conformist leadership persona of a large state-owned company, notwithstanding his young age of 39 when he took over as chief executive. For instance, when Walsh became CEO, he evaded the flamboyant ceremony and got down to work very quickly. Many of his colleagues have highlighted his passion for his work by describing him as an early bird who arrives at Aer Lingus headquarters by 8.00a.m. and begins the day by personally checking his e-mails. He has no personal assistant and prefers to control his own diary. Some would also describe him as a risk taker, by transforming a high premium price airline into a low-fares one over such a short period of time. This high-risk taking highlights the entrepreneurial spirit and leadership instinct that he possesses. His entrepreneurial personality is personified by his having an astute eye for opportunity and a good hand at bargaining.

An Entrepreneurial Leader and 'The Survival Plan'

Aer Lingus looked to be heading for trouble post September 11th with a possible take-over being regarded by many commentators as the best, indeed the only, option to secure a future for the airline. However, the events of September 11th precipitated an extraordinary change in the overall business climate of Aer Lingus. What could have been a disaster for the company instead became a chance to shift position in the competitive airline market. A youthful visionary, Walsh saw an opportunity that needed to be exploited and developed it. He rapidly set about implementing a new formula for competing.

Overhauling structure and strategy

The group redefined its mission statement, asserting the need to achieve sustained profitability through commercially viable products and practices involving a keen customer focus. The idea of 'keen customer focus' had been embedded within the Aer Lingus ethos from the very start of the company's history. They developed a reputation for friendliness and service, enabling them to win countless accolades over the years.[9] It was precisely this that Walsh desired to exploit and build on while providing low prices to enhance the average perceived value of the customer when compared with other low cost airlines.[10]

With the strategic intent of building on low prices with consistent quality in service, Walsh began by immediately halving the business-class fares that had been the premise of the airline's life as a flag carrier. For instance, the airline's premium return fare from Dublin to Brussels was lowered from €1,000 to €498.[11] At the same time, Walsh realised that the yield had duly tumbled, causing a 7 per cent fall in revenues along the way. But he stood by his new business model, arguing that it was a more accurate picture of what the real underlying demand was for a full business product. Walsh never doubted that the low-cost sector was here to stay and he consequently began to benchmark very assertively against low-cost airlines. In the past, Aer Lingus used to benchmark against traditional flag carriers. Walsh came to grips with the reality that the carrier was being driven by the customer, doing what they wanted and prepared to pay for it, whereas in the past, the focus was less on customer needs and more on providing elaborate service. As a result, the company reduced the confusion within the firm and this helped bring overall costs down by 30 per cent. Accordingly, the highest on the list of savings was in sales and distribution, which was weighing in at a hefty 56 per cent of turnover. The smart benchmarking by the executive team had demonstrated that Aer Lingus was at a monolithic cost disadvantage against Ryanair, representing more than €20 per passenger per sector.[12] Bearing in mind the colossal cost in sales and distribution, Walsh focused his time and efforts on cutting travel agency commission and thereafter he increased his efforts in promoting the Aer Lingus flight booking website. In an interview he stated:

> Providing a better Internet service was a direct response to what the customer wanted. The internet brings transparency, it allows customers to look for, and achieve, good value, while sitting at their own computer.[13]

In just two years, internet bookings climbed to more than half of all ticket sales. By 2004, 40 per cent of tickets sales outside the Irish market were made over the web and the figure stood at over 60 per cent at home, across all services and tickets. The figures represented over €1 million of revenue per day by mid-2004. Walsh wants to take the online share up to around the 70 per cent mark and this could increase in the long-run with the increase in the adoption of UMTS mobile commerce platforms. Aer Lingus still handles 10–12 per cent of sales through call centres and will keep some business fares available on the computer reservation system.

The new model that Walsh adopted was one of catering for all sides of the aviation market. Essentially, the new Aer Lingus model had some aspects of the Ryanair model but it was not a pure low-cost carrier, as it was still providing an elevated quality of service, for which they were renowned. Walsh believed that not moving with the swift change in trends could be hazardous to any business that was reluctant to change. Hence, with this in mind Walsh decided Aer Lingus must have a twin track strategy, namely to offer cheaper fares while maintaining a reputation as a 'full service' airline, where appropriate. Moreover, he believed that the key to success lay not in providing an elaborate service but in being consistent. In tandem with this, the company continued its cost-reduction initiatives and fare reductions. Walsh took the view that it was more important to fly to destinations where customers wanted to go, rather than where a legacy route existed. He added 30 new routes to the airline's European network, closing four historic loss-makers, and experimented with new, often leisure-driven services. An example of the new routes was from Dublin to the Spanish mass-market beach resort of Malaga, routes with which the old Aer Lingus would never have been associated. This route expansion has emerged as one area in which Aer Lingus is trumping Ryanair. The state carrier has cleverly exploited the fact that Ryanair has refused to develop new routes out of Dublin, due to a long-running dispute between Ryanair and the Irish airport authority (Aer Rianta) over landing charges and the building of a second terminal at Dublin Airport. This has virtually left the field open to Aer Lingus in terms of new route development from Dublin.

As part of the survival plan, the senior management team sought to emphasise the points of difference that give the carrier an edge in terms of service. These include four simple key benefits: friendly service, assigned seating, flights direct to main airports and the promise never to leave the passenger stranded. He stipulated in an interview that advertising in the past may have focused on the luxury of business travellers but that was no longer viable and realistic.[14] In the past, Aer Lingus promised more than they could deliver but now they deliver what is needed. Despite some criticism, Walsh believes his new business model of quality service and consistency, allied with cheap fares, can win over the doubters by creating greater perceived value than their competitors in the eyes of the consumer. If you can offer free intangibles by allowing people to take extra hand luggage onboard – space permitting – at no extra cost, it will indirectly increase the perceived value of their product. Furthermore, if a customer misses their flight or faces a cancellation, they can get the next available flight without any extra cost. Such service propositions increase the perceived value for the customer, which increases brand loyalty and overall revenues (see Appendix 9.1).

REINVENTION AT AER LINGUS: WALSH'S 'TRIPLE A' APPROACH

The Walsh re-invention strategy had three components, which can be classified as the 'triple A's approach':[15] *Acceptance* of the changing environment, *Action* phase, *Adherence* and consistency in value creation.

Acceptance approach

Nearly every carrier worldwide has tasted the reality of deflated earnings after 2001: the terrorist attacks in Indonesia, war in Afghanistan, war in Iraq and SARS. Many airlines in Europe and in the US were slow to comprehend the scope of the calamity that was developing. But Walsh grasped that this time things were different and the distinct factors that had been building for some time had finally reached a point of no return. He correctly assumed and accepted that bankruptcy was a very real possibility, after Swissair and Sabena failed. In accordance with understanding the market environment, Walsh did something that none of his European or American peers did: he benchmarked against the real competition, Ryanair, rather than against the other legacy carriers. Unlike, for instance, United Airlines, which set Delta's costs as its benchmark, Walsh correctly perceived that they had to re-position themselves in the market and modify their business model, if they were to avoid the usual pattern of reaching a targeted goal only to find that the savings were insufficient and the process was to be restarted. Unlike almost everyone else, Walsh perceived that the new model had to focus not on the traditional competitors, but on the low-cost airlines that posed the greatest threat to the survival of Aer Lingus. Commenting on the turnaround strategy he stated:

> ... the survival plan is only the beginning of a process of cost-cutting. What we have to do is become more efficient. We're questioning every single aspect of our cost base and where we can identify costs that can be cut out, we will do so, and give it back to the customer in the form of low fares.[16]

Action approach

The acceptance led to an instant reaction. The program was more rigorous and had a lot more substance than anything undertaken by Aer Lingus' competitors. The implementation and timing were correctly executed by Walsh, unlike many of his competitors. There were no half-measures undertaken and the transformation that was begun was designed to deal with essentials rather than a singular downturn. These strategic actions included:[17]

- Cost reduction of €190 million, 16 per cent of this achieved through reducing staff by 2,000 or 40 per cent of the total
- Booking costs reduction of 40 per cent as online booking increased and 1 per cent reduction in commissions to travel agents[18]
- Pay freeze for pilots until February 2003
- Reduction in leisure fares of more than 50 per cent
- Increase capacity at these fares to over 50 per cent
- Reduction in business fares of more than 50 per cent
- Realignment of capacity with demand to stimulate traffic
- Revenue management focus shifted to load factor
- Commission reductions
- Fleet reductions and increased utilisation
- Concentration on direct web marketing.

These actions needed the support of everyone in the organisation, a difficult challenge considering the impact that it was going to have on many different sectors of the company.

Adherence and consistency approach

Lastly, and most significantly, Aer Lingus fully embraced the idea that this new model was not a one-off event but an ongoing strategic process, constantly dynamic and never complacent. One of the points often repeated was the fact that the actions already taken were only the opening rounds of an ongoing battle to reduce cost, maintain quality and increase efficiency. As was pointed out repeatedly by the CEO, in a competitive market you have to keep business simple. In the past, the company, to its detriment, was guilty of confusing complexity with quality. This needed to change if they were to deal with the threat of the low-cost carrier.[19]

The Aer Lingus top management team freely admits that their current position is still short of being fully competitive with Ryanair. However, they have a clear vision of that gap and a strategy to cope with its presence. The first aspect is to continue to reduce their costs and narrow the differential. The other part of the strategic plan is to create additional value in the Aer Lingus brand, giving substance to any fare differentials that may exist. Especially important to Aer Lingus is the customer service component, a point at which they judge Ryanair to be most exposed.

Changing the corporate culture inevitably proved the most significant challenge. Radical downsizing always creates fear and uncertainty, but one of the interesting obstacles was the purposeful use of the word 'cheap' to describe the new Aer Lingus product. Seen often as a desirable attribute from the customer perspective, internally it unleashed all the negative connotations and associations that network carriers associate with the low-cost segment. Other changes were equally suspect. Aer Lingus had previously, like most traditional carriers, entered new markets only after substantive study and anticipating a development curve, begun at a loss, with a two- to three-year period allowed for route profitability. Clearly, few airlines are any longer in a position to move so slowly towards profitability. Aer Lingus abandoned this established route development plan and simply inaugurated services to new, promising destinations – most clearly outside the established Aer Lingus pattern.

CORPORATE REVIVAL

The ultimate proof of the turnaround strategy came after the implementation of the survival plan that saw a return to profits. It was evident that the announced plans to layoff 40 per cent (2,000 redundancies) of its workforce and reduce its cost by €190 million[20] ($186.7 million) was justified. Aer Lingus had turned in operating profits of €64 million ($82 million) for 2002, equivalent to a margin of 6.6 per cent on revenues that had dipped just under €1 billion.[21] For 2003, that had risen to just over €75 million, a margin approaching double figures. Walsh's focus on costs made the airline leaner, more flexible and more competitive. In approximately six months, Walsh turned a significant loss into an altogether unexpected profit. He stated in an interview that:

> I fully recognize the trauma that this will cause many staff members and their families over the coming weeks, and I am saddened that we have to embark on such a course of action ... But trading prospects are bright and Aer Lingus now seems better positioned than ever to take on the competition, including the 'low-price' operators.[22]

It is the positioning that needed most attention, as it was precisely the cutting of costs and attention in service delivery that assisted Aer Lingus to their good fortune.[23]

Recently, Willie Walsh argued that while the company has made huge progress, its competitors do not stop moving forward. They have also made progress. Therefore if Aer Lingus stops progressing, it may take two or three years, but Aer Lingus will be back in crisis. Willie Walsh is not the kind of person who wants to be in a business that slowly descends back into a crisis.

DEALING WITH FUTURE CHANGE IN THE AIRLINE INDUSTRY

According to the EU Transport Commissioner, Loyola De Palacio, there is going to be a reorganisation of the aviation sector in Europe as the continent stops thinking in terms of national carriers. It is likely that pan-EU, rather than individual country, ownership will become the norm and the European Commission, rather than national governments, will negotiate traffic rights starting with EU and US bilateral agreements. Furthermore, the world of the small state protected national flag carriers is likely to disappear forever. Consolidation has swept through most industries in the western world, but because of their status as national standard bearers, it has so far eluded the legacy airlines. Major consolidation in the global airline industry appears to be underway. If this happens and should Aer Lingus ever be floated successfully, there is a distinct possibility that it will be ultimately taken over by a large carrier. Aer Lingus is a small peripheral player in global terms, although its business could prove attractive to a North American airline keen to use it as a hub into Europe. As such, the current environment will continue to be a cause of uncertainty. Deregulation will spread to regions of the world hitherto untouched. The ownership rule requiring airlines to be substantially owned and effectively controlled by nationals of their country of registration will be under pressure and is likely to be progressively abandoned. In Europe, the 2004 expansion of the European civil aviation area to encompass an additional ten states creates new opportunities and threats for many of Europe's airlines. The airlines of the new member states, largely government owned, face the full force of open and free competition domestically and internationally for the first time. However, Ireland as an island community is restricted to air and sea transport for its foreign travel, conferring added advantages for the airline industry in Ireland. The current frenzy for alliances will continue. Old partners may be abandoned and new partnerships created. The industry will move from an era of concentration to an era of consolidation.

The key issues facing the industry appear to be the rate of return in traffic growth, the potential return of pricing power and the opportunity for restructuring the airlines for the longer term. Overall, a climate of continuous change and uncertainty faces many leaders in this industry. What business model can best meet the challenges ahead? The traditional airline model is that of a business that provides in-house most of the services and functions it requires. Aer Lingus' departmental structure reflects this. There were, and still are, separate departments dealing with engineering and overhaul, in-flight catering, ground handling, cargo, reservations and ticketing, sales, IT and so on. All of these functions are considered so important and critical for the efficient running of the business that airline managements have felt they had to control them directly. For Aer Lingus and other flag carriers, this will have to change as it is now becoming more cost-effective to outsource these areas of activity.

Due to Aer Lingus' recent financial and structural problems, CEO Willie Walsh has looked towards both the Ryanair model of how to run a modern airline and facets of British Airways' premium blueprint. Aer Lingus has begun to implement many of these characteristics into their own strategies by providing lower fares, reducing the workforce by 2,000 people to cut costs and developing their internet capabilities to provide for internet sales. All of these were undertaken whilst simultaneously maintaining their premium service and branding integrity.

AER LINGUS – LOOKING TO THE FUTURE

Given the scale and nature of change that has already been achieved by Walsh, most network carrier top management teams would consider the goals achieved and concentrate instead on stabilising the organisation and focusing on outcomes. However, that response, repeated constantly over the past decades, is not a part of the new model that constantly attempts to simplify, reduce and align itself with the market that is determining the revenue. Immediately on the horizon are the following initiatives that Aer Lingus and Walsh plan to focus on: [24]

- *Creation of consistent brand value*: Currently the average Aer Lingus European sector flight is priced at €63, compared with Ryanair at €49. As stated earlier, Aer Lingus does not anticipate parity but hopes to create additional value, corresponding in the customer's mind to the fare differential. The premium is to be service-based, focused on service features that do not add to cost.
- *Attainment of a margin of 15 per cent*: The turnaround profit in 2002

represented a 6 per cent margin. The goal is to increase that 2.5 times.

- *Establishment of a new benchmark of customer value*: Current mileage programs, while popular with customers, have never been especially good at determining true customer value. Aer Lingus intends to capture and use customer data to determine passenger value and then alter the way in which it rewards its best customers. This will in the long run help build strong relationships with its customers.

- *Continuous improvement of online booking facility*: The current 40 per cent is scheduled to move to 50 per cent and to that end they have targeted an improvement in the added value capacity of the site, further cost reductions and the channelling of other business (such as direct corporate access) to the site. Additionally the company plans to continuously upgrade the help facilities and improve error handling.

Bearing in mind the notion of value creation, Walsh will face challenges to sustain a strong strategic architecture but he will also look at the options of raising the ancillary revenue. Ryanair has made significant profits from selling everything from car hire and hotel rooms to travel insurance. First, the question needs to be asked whether Aer Lingus will follow a similar pathway to provide more value in the eyes of the customer. The competition is already braced for such a move:

> ... in the face of stiffer competition, O'Leary will try to meet his opponents head-on and out-low-fare them all. He has built up an impressive war chest (€1.15 billion in the bank) and might be intent to sacrifice profit growth for market share. [25]

The company also needs to finalise some unfinished business with regard to the group's privatisation. Aer Lingus has been on the list for the best part of a decade, but governments have come and gone without any progress. Finally, Aer Lingus needs to maintain security and the confidence of the travelling public, efficient management practices working on the basis of sound human resource principles, a competitive workforce and a product that the public want and are willing to pay for across the spectrum of demand. This list is by no means exhaustive and is only the tip of the iceberg. The people who work and invest in Aer Lingus are key to its survival, a point not lost on the CEO:

> All our staff deserve great credit. They acknowledged the enormity

of the situation and faced up to the challenges. We have come through a crisis unlike anything we had in the past.[26]

KEEP IT SIMPLE: THE 'WALSH WAY'

There is little doubt that the airline business is changing rapidly and that carriers must evolve or risk extinction. The past and ongoing challenges that Walsh faces will inspire future entrepreneurial leaders that want to reinvent their companies. Walsh, the value revolutionary, aims to ensure that premium traffic and the attitudes to network planning have changed. The era that relied on routes that were driven only by the business market are coming to an end. A number of services will have business class entirely stripped out and it will only be retained where it is adding real value rather than just complexity. Walsh's vision aims for a much more sustainable balance by offering low prices and quality in service at no extra cost. But these are substantial goals, to be achieved by a leaner workforce with a (once again) growing network. Profitability and the stunning progress already made are powerful incentives to staff and stakeholders. Aer Lingus and Walsh are successfully remaking their company using a new model and it is working. With cash in hand and profits growing, there is less urgency than when he took the helm and the top management team is not in any hurry to have to deal with the distraction that a market flotation would bring. For now the target is to keep driving costs down, focusing on the core product and building the company for further growth. Charles Darwin famously remarked that in the evolutionary race, it is not necessarily the strongest that survive but the most adaptable. If Willie Walsh has his way, Aer Lingus will not only survive but will thrive. Under his leadership, the state carrier has not only avoided a crash landing – it has successfully taken off again. The future holds many challenges but Walsh has proved that he is adept at finding creative solutions.

NOTES

1. This case is intended to be used as the basis for class discussion rather than to illustrate either effective or ineffective handling of a management situation.
2. Denis Harrington is a Lecturer in Strategy and Leadership at Waterford Institute of Technology. Thomas Lawton is Senior Lecturer in Strategy and International Business and Tazeeb Rajwani is a Researcher in Strategic Management at Imperial College, London.
3. http://www.aviationnow.com/avnow/search/xml/aviationdaily_xml/2002/08/02/14.xml –26/01/04
4. Lourdes, in the south of France, is a major center of pilgrimage for Roman

Catholics. 1950s Ireland was a devoutly Catholic country and Lourdes was therefore an obvious choice for one of Aer Lingus' first routes.

5. The collapse of GPA in 1993 took Aer Lingus to the brink of bankruptcy.

6. David McWilliams (2001) 'Don't Pay Twice for Aer Lingus', *Sunday Business Post*, 21 October.

7. Aer Lingus Annual Report, 2001.

8. Kevin O'Toole (2004) 'A New Vision', *Airline Business*, March, p. 27.

9. Aer Lingus won three categories in the annual business travel readers' awards: best transatlantic airline, best Ireland-Europe airline and best frequent flyer program. Furthermore, they also won the new Phoenix Award for reinventing themselves as a low-cost airline.

10. O'Toole, op cit.

11. Willie Walsh CEO, Aer Lingus, Telecommunication and Internet federation report – 'A New Beginning', 23 October 2003, p. 7.

12. O'Toole, op cit.

13. M. O'Brien (2002) 'How Aer Lingus Turned it around', *Sunday Business Post*, 29 September.

14. O'Toole, op. cit.

15. http://www.unisys.com/

16. *Business and Finance Magazine* (2003) 'Walsh's Turnaround', 30 November.

17. http://www.Aerlingus.com

18. http://www.airlinequality.com/news/Aer Lingus.htm, 16/01/04.

19. N. Connolly (2002) 'Walsh Knocks Aer Lingus into Shape', *Sunday Business Post*, 4 August.

20. http://www.atwonline.com, from Air Transport World website, 'Aer Lingus reports heavy loss for 2001, cites progress in 2002', Thursday 1 August 2002.

21. O'Toole, op cit., p. 28.

22. 'Aer Lingus names Walsh CEO, plans to cut 32 per cent of employees', http//www.aviationnnow.com/avnow/search/xml/aviationdaily_xml/archive/AD102201_2. 26/01/2004.

23. http://www.unisys.com/

24. IMI Management Conference, 'Back to Basics Survive and Thrive', Aer Lingus, 2003.

25. D. McWilliams (2004) 'Magic Bus Generation Holds Key for Ryanair', *Sunday Business Post*, 2 January.

26. O'Brien, op. cit.

27. http://www.Aerlingus.com, company news.

28. Willie Walsh CEO, Aer Lingus, Telecommunication and internet federation report - A new beginning, 23 October 2003.

Appendix 9.1: **Customer Service Statistics of complaints for 2003**

Lost Bag Complaints per 1,000 Passengers:

January	1.34
February	0.85
March	1.01
April	0.87

Passenger Complaints per 1,000 Passengers:

January	1.91
February	1.04
March	0.91
April	0.89

Passenger Complaints per 1,000 Passengers:

Week ending	On time	Within 60 minutes
18/05/03	87%	99%
11/05/03	91%	99%
04/05/03	86%	99%
27/04/03	87%	98%
20/04/03	87%	98%
13/04/03	86%	99%

Source: Aer Lingus-Year 2003[27]

Appendix 9.2: **Aer Lingus Select Statistics**

Operation	Change
Seat capacity	-6%
Passenger traffic	7%
Load factor	**+11pt**
Yield	-23%
Unit cost	-35%
Selected costs	
Distribution	-56%
Aircraft	-51%
Overheads	-36%
Airport fees	-28%
Staff costs	-21
Maintenance	-12%
Total costs	**-30%**

Source: O'Toole, op cit., p. 29.
Note: Change through to November 2003.

Appendix 9.3: **Change in the Business Model**

2003 versus 2001	
Change in overall capacity	-6%
Change in passenger traffic	7
Change in passenger load factor	+11 points
Change in average fares	-24%
Change in unit costs	-35%
Change in distribution cost	-56%

Source: Telecommunication and Internet federation report 2003[28]

Appendix 9.4: **Financial Highlights**
for the year ended 31 December 2003

	2003 **€ million**	2002 € million	2001 € million
Profit and loss			
Turnover – Continuing operations	**888.3**	958.6	1,097.2
Operating costs	**805.3**	894.8	1,149.3
Operating profit (loss) (1)	**83.0**	63.8	(52.1)
Operating margin (%)	**9.3%**	6.7%	(4.7%)
EBITDAR (2)	**186.9**	176.8	104.3
Net exceptional cost	**–**	(25.7)	(104.1)
Profit (loss) for the year	**69.2**	35.3	(139.9)
Earnings (loss) per share (€ cent)	**27.1c**	13.8c	(54.7c)
Balance sheet			
Shareholders' funds	**321.9**	255.6	223.9
Free cash	**384.8**	367.3	169.5
Net cash and liquid resources (3)	**226.2**	154.9	66.0
Key statistics – Continuing operations			
Passengers flown (scheduled)	**6,594,650**	6,210,891	6,307,371
Passenger load factor (flown %)	**81%**	78%	71%
Premium class bookings (%)	**7%**	10%	13%
Average flown fare – Europe (€)	**82.52**	92.32	103.10
Average sector length – Europe (kms)	**727**	639	597
Average flown fare – Transatlantic (€)	**250.97**	316.04	327.77
Average sector length – Transatlantic (kms)	**5,517**	5,548	5,547
Average number of aircraft operated	**32.9**	32.8	37.2
Average number of employees	**4,281**	4,650	6,108
Internet sales at year-end	**50%**	28%	8%

(1) Operating profit on continuing operations before employee profit share.
(2) Earnings on continuing operations before employee profit share, interest, tax, depreciation, amortisation and aircraft rentals.
(3) Free cash plus restricted cash deposits less finance lease obligations and debt.

Source: Aer Lingus – Annual Report 2003

Appendix 9.5: **Consolidated Profit and Loss Account for year ended 31 December 2003***

	Notes	2003 €000	2002 Continuing Operations €000	Discontinued Operations €000	Total €000
Turnover	1	**888,298**	958,650	212,286	1,170,936
Cost of sales	1	**(651,598)**	(692,195)	(201,775)	(893,970)
Gross profit		**236,700**	266,455	10,511	276,966
Other operating expenses					
– operating	1	**(153,735)**	(202,609)	(1,292)	(203,901)
– employee profit share	20	**(8,822)**	(7,511)	–	(7,511)
– employee profit share (exceptional)	2	–	1,577	–	1,577
		(162,557)	(208,543)	(1,292)	(209,835)
Operating profit	1	**74,143**	57,912	9,219	67,131
Exceptional items					
Cost of fundamental restructuring	2	–	(71,239)	–	(71,239)
Profit on disposal of fixed assets and investments	2	–	26,970	–	26,970
Profit on exit from non-core activities	2	–	–	12,089	12,089
Profit on ordinary activities before interest		**74,143**	13,643	21,308	34,951
Interest receivable and similar income		**32,592**	30,619	541	31,160
Interest payable and similar charges	3	**(27,332)**	(29,116)	–	(29,116)
Profit on ordinary activities before taxation	4	**79,403**	15,146	21,849	36,995
Taxation	7	**(10,186)**	1,687	(2,949)	(1,262)
Profit on ordinary activities after taxation		**69,217**	16,833	18,900	35,733
Minority interests	18	-	-	(418)	(418)
Profit for the year		**68,217**	16,833	18,482	35,315
Earnings per share (€ cent)	8	**27.1c**			13.8c
Earnings per share – continuing operations before exceptional items (€ cent)	8	**27.1c**			21.3c

*All of the results for 2003 are derived from continuing operations.
Source: Aer Lingus – Annual Report 2003

Aer Lingus

....

Appendix 9.6

Income Statement	Dec 01	Dec 00	Dec 99
Revenue	1,193.5	1,292.3	1,216.1
Cost of Goods Sold	968.4	913.6	830.3
Gross Profit	225.1	378.7	385.9
Gross Profit Margin	18.9%	29.3%	31.7%
SG&A Expense	269.7	303.4	289.3
Depreciation & Amortization	--	--	--
Operating Income	(44.6)	75.3	96.5
Operating Margin	--	5.8%	7.9%
Nonoperating Income	42.1	12.5	--
Nonoperating Expenses	136.6	11.8	36.6
Income Before Taxes	(139.1)	83.9	60.0
Income Taxes	(15.7)	15.9	6.3
Net Income After Taxes	(123.4)	68.0	53.7
Continuing Operations	--	--	--
Discontinued Operations	--	--	--
Total Operations	--	--	--
Total Net Income	(123.9)	67.4	52.3
Net Profit Margin	--	5.2%	4.3%

Source: Hoovers.com-2004

Financial Overview	2001	2000	1999	1998
Annual Sales ($ mil.)	1,193.5	1,292.3	1,216.1	1,341.8
Annual Net Income ($ mil.)	(123.9)	67.4	52.3	79.9

Source: Hoovers.com-2004

Appendix 9.7

Balance Sheet	Dec 01	Dec 00	Dec 99
Assets			
Current Assets			
Cash	555.0	777.1	766.5
Net Receivables	96.1	116.1	130.2
Inventories	5.9	7.0	6.7
Other Current Assets	0.0	--	--
Total Current Assets	657.0	900.2	903.4
Net Fixed Assets	638.8	578.4	544.9
Other Noncurrent Assets	0.0	--	--
Total Assets	**1,295.8**	**1,479.4**	**1,448.3**

Liabilities and Shareholders' Equity			
Current Liabilities			
Accounts Payable	45.3	60.0	--
Short-Term Debt	92.1	38.2	431.6
Other Current Liabilities	--	--	--
Total Current Liabilities	432.9	489.8	431.6
Long-Term Debt	404.5	430.6	511.1
Other Noncurrent Liabilities	--	25.3	203.6
Total Liabilities	**1,097.5**	**1,134.1**	**1,146.3**

Cash Flow Statement	Dec 01	Dec 00	Dec 99
Net Operating Cash Flow	--	--	--
Net Investing Cash Flow	--	--	--
Net Financing Cash Flow	--	--	--
Net Change in Cash	--	--	--
Depreciation & Amortization	--	--	--
Capital Expenditures	--	--	--
Cash Dividends Paid	--	--	--

Appendix 9.8

Income Statement				
Year	Revenue ($ mil.)	NetIncome ($ mil.)	NetProfit Margin	Employees
Dec 01	1,193.5	(123.9)	--	6,833
Dec 00	1,292.3	67.4	5.2%	6,624
Dec 99	1,216.1	52.3	4.3%	7,044
Dec 98	1,341.8	79.9	6.0%	8,316
Dec 97	1,143.2	(65.4)	--	8,308
Dec 96	1,295.6	54.1	4.2%	8,416
Dec 95	1,273.0	24.2	1.9%	--
Dec 94	1,283.5	--	--	--
Dec 93	1,172.1	--	--	

2001 Year-End Financials	
Debt Ratio	--
Cash ($ mil.)	555.0
Current Ratio	1.52
Long-Term Debt ($ mil.)	404.5

10

The Special Olympics 2003[1]

PAULINE CONNOLLY and GERALDINE McGING[2]

Let me win, but if I cannot win, let me be brave in the attempt.

On 21 June 2003, the spectacular opening ceremony of the world's biggest sporting event of 2003 took place in Ireland. This followed an arduous task of strategic planning and organisation that first started in 1995. With the support of the Irish government, a proposal was put to Special Olympics International for Ireland to host the games and in 1999 Ireland was awarded the Games. The Special Olympics World Summer Games 2003 is a story of entrepreneurship, vision and commitment. It is also an account of project planning, organisation and teamwork at an exceptionally high level. This is the story of those Games.

The Games were organised by Special Olympics World Summer Games 2003 Limited. This newly established company raised a total of €60 million in sponsorship, of which €36 million was cash and €24 million was products and services that were donated in kind. With the assistance of over 30,000 volunteers and the hospitality of 1,000 host families, the country played host to over 7,000 athletes, 3,000 coaches and official delegates and 28,000 family members and friends over a two-week period. In addition to the financial success of hosting the games, The Post Games Network (with the slogan 'there's a place for everyone') was created, which highlights positive attitudes towards people with learning disabilities. Their slogan remains an encouraging and optimistic legacy of the success of maintaining positive attitudes towards individuals with intellectual disabilities.

SPECIAL OLYMPICS

Special Olympics is an international organisation dedicated to empowering individuals with intellectual disabilities to become physically fit, productive and respected members of society through sports training and competition.

SPECIAL OLYMPICS MISSION

The mission of Special Olympics is a simple one: to encourage people with a learning disability to reach their full potential through the benefits of participating in sport. At the same time, the Special Olympics work to engender positive public attitudes towards a population that is often rejected or forgotten. The Special Olympics started in 1963 in the United States when Eunice Kennedy Schriver started a summer camp for people with learning difficulties. Five years later the First International Special Olympics Summer Games took place in Chicago. Until 2003, the games were never hosted outside of the United States. Following the huge success of the Games in Ireland, the organisation's goal now is to increase the number of athletes participating worldwide to two million by 2005.

SPECIAL OLYMPICS IRELAND

Special Olympics Ireland is the national governing body for sport for people with a learning disability in Ireland. The organisation was established in 1978 and it has been sending athletes to compete in the Special Olympics since 1979. Special Olympics Ireland is organised into four regions, Connaught, Leinster, Munster and Northern Ireland. Throughout these regions there is approximately 450 Special Olympics schools, centres, workshops and clubs. Of the 35,000 individuals with a learning disability in Ireland (including Northern Ireland), 8,000 are currently involved in Special Olympics Ireland. Special Olympics Ireland is proactive in promoting and implementing the mission, vision and goals of the Special Olympics, whilst also promoting their own aims.

The ultimate aim is for a dynamic, professional organisation which is athlete centred and community based while maintaining its voluntary ethos.

SPECIAL OLYMPICS IRELAND STRATEGY 2004–2007

HOW IRELAND WON THE GAMES

In 1995, the founders of the games were approached about the possibility of the Games being held outside of the United States for the first time since their inception. Later that year the Board of Special Olympics International decided on an open bidding process for the Games. In June 1996, the Irish government established an interdepartmental group to examine the feasibility of Ireland hosting the games and in November 1997, Ireland's bid was submitted to the Board. On 31 March 1999, at a prestigious state reception in the Royal Hospital, Kilmainham, the President of the Special Olympics, Timothy Shriver, announced that Ireland had won the bid for the 2003 World Summer Games. Among the guests at the event were An Taoiseach, the Lord Mayor of Dublin and the US ambassador. It was the successful culmination of a four-year intensive competitive process. According to Mary Davis, CEO of the Special Olympics World Summer Games 2003, three factors contributed to Ireland winning the bid. Firstly, Special Olympics Ireland already enjoyed a strong reputation for its support of the Special Olympics programme. Secondly, the hosting of the Games could not succeed without a significant input of volunteer labour and Ireland had a long-established tradition of voluntary and community effort. Thirdly, the Irish government was very supportive of the bid: they lobbied hard and made an initial financial commitment of €6.35 million and made a further commitment to provide a world-class Olympic-sized swimming pool, which was subsequently built at the National Aquatic Centre at Abbotstown.

MANAGEMENT STRUCTURE: WORLD SUMMER GAMES 2003 LTD

The success of the 2003 Special Olympics Games can be attributed to two factors: firstly, an effective management structure that changed and evolved to meet the needs of a dynamic and developing organisation; secondly, a highly motivated and entrepreneurial team of staff and volunteers. In 2000, a Council of Patrons, headed up by An Taoiseach, provided the organisation with much needed initial support from a range of high profile committed individuals. The Games Organising Committee (GOC) operated as a company through the name Special Olympics World Summer Games 2003 Limited. Under the Chairmanship of Denis O'Brien, and with Mary Davis as the Chief Executive Officer, the GOC was established as a company limited by guarantee and not having share capital. As the planning for the event progressed, the management structure changed to meet the needs of the developing company (see Appendix 10.1 and 10.2). An executive office was established, led by Mary Davis, which took over from the GOC and the Board and had primary responsibility for the strategic planning, the operations and implementation of the plans.

MARY DAVIS: CHIEF EXECUTIVE OFFICER

Mary Davis is married with four children. She qualified as a physical education teacher and was appointed as a physical education co-ordinator with St Michael's House in Dublin, an organisation catering for people with learning disabilities. While there, she became involved as a volunteer with Special Olympics Ireland. In 1985 she was events director for the European Special Olympics Games that were held in Dublin. Two thousand athletes from fifteen countries took part. Following these Games, she was appointed Chairperson of Special Olympics Ireland and in 1989 she became the Chief Executive of that organisation. During this time, the work of Special Olympics in Ireland flourished and in 1995 Davis successfully led Ireland's bid to host the Special Olympics World Games. On the occasion of the conferring of the Degree of Doctorate of Laws, honoris causa on Mary Davis, An Dr I. Ó Muircheartaigh (2004) paid tribute to Davis and said that 'It was her vision, leadership and determination that mobilised the effort into spectacular success which was the 2003 World Games'.

Davis has also been honoured with an honorary degree from Dublin City University, Taltler Magazine's International Woman of the Year, Electricity Supply Board's/Rehab Irish Person of the Year Award 2003, O2 Professional and Business Woman – Special Award, Marketer of the Year – Marketing Magazine in association with Edelman, The Sunday Independent Person of the Month, and she was also awarded the Renault Sports Star Award. Currently she serves on many committees and boards including The Irish Sports Council, The Broadcasting Commission of Ireland, European Year of Education through Sport and she also chairs the St Patrick's Festival.

BUILDING THE TEAM

The composition of the management team was crucial. It was important that the team was in a position to 'open doors' and gain support as the fund-raising effort was going to be central to the financial viability of the Games. The GOC's Board of Directors comprised of 22 experienced and skilled individuals with backgrounds in entertainment, politics, industry and the public sector, and included names such as Eddie Jordan (Formula 1 team owner), Pat Kenny (broadcaster, RTE), P.J. Mara (Chief Executive, Mara Associates), Joe McDonagh (former President GAA), Ronan Keating (singer) and Marjorie (Mo) Mowlam (former Secretary of State of

Northern Ireland). Denis O' Brien, who chaired the board, was a highly successful entrepreneur in his own right, and Mary Davis (CEO) had a wealth of experience in managing sporting events and in dealing with people with learning difficulties.

Management consultants were invited from the United States to meet with the management team at a summit in Belfast to provide strategic advice on brand building, corporate sponsorship and sales. This meeting provided an excellent forum for the management team to discuss their mission and to focus their strategies. The importance of effective teamwork, leadership and communication took on a heightened edge as the organisation grew and developed. Departments were set up in order to respond to the emerging needs of the company and the customer, i.e. the athletes, sponsors and general public. Nine departments were set up (see Appendix 10.1 and 10.2), including Sports and Competition, Fundraising, Business Operations, Support Services and Volunteers, Special Events, Ceremonies, International Services and Communications (including the Marketing Function). A Chief Financial Officer supported these departments. The team had, according to Mary Davis, 'One Goal, One Team and One Chance' to make this event a success.

Throughout the planning stage, senior management remained focused on the company's objectives and as a result the original plans changed and developed in response to the evolving needs of the organisation. For example, in 2003, the Special Olympics World Summer Games 2003 Limited organised the European National Games, which was attended by 2,000 athletes. They viewed this as an opportunity to identify weaknesses or flaws in their planning and operations for the World Games. It enabled them also to explore how the organisation would deal with transport issues and language difficulties, and gave the teams an opportunity to gain a practical feel of the event. As a result of this, plans, departments and teams were changed. Mary Davis acknowledged that, while this process was not without its difficulties, it enabled the cross-fertilisation of ideas and gave staff the opportunity to work in new teams.

Communication and planning, Davis states, were key positive forces at this stage, making sure that everyone on the team knew what they were supposed to be doing and what other people were doing. At times, however, this was difficult as the organisation had three locations around Dublin and people had to move between different floors of one building and at times had to move between different buildings to attend meetings and presentations. The teams were also continually revising and updating their plans to meet the changing needs of the organisation.

All methods of communications were used throughout the planning stages and while communication at times was a challenge, it was also central to the effective planning of the Games. The organisation expanded to employ 280 people and they were supported by a volunteer team of 30,000 people located throughout Ireland. The Games website and all official publications were updated in a timely manner as and when they were required to meet the needs and expectations of all participants in the Games, including internal departments and other interested parties. Furthermore, the Games premier sponsor, Bank of Ireland, updated their intranet on a daily basis to allow employees to follow all the developments.

While the Games ran smoothly, this did not happen by accident and it was a true reflection of the meticulous planning that was undertaken by the organisation and by the departments and teams that worked on the event. For example, contingency planning and risk management were explored in detail. Emergency plans were put in place to deal with any emergency or crisis should they arise, such as food poisoning or illness. The team even simulated two emergencies to assess the effectiveness of their contingency planning. A bomb scare was announced in Croke Park with the opening ceremony just hours away, and, at the same time, a coach carrying athletes to an event had a serious accident on the M50. This enabled the teams to put their various plans into operation and to assess how feasible these plans would be to implement should a need arise.

MARKETING

In order for the Games to be successful, marketing was to play a very important role in the overall strategy for success. The marketing efforts and raising of finance were highly interdependent upon each other and ultimately the Games' success. Because of this the company needed creative marketing professionals to work on their marketing campaign, specialists who would be able to create media messages that would appeal to sponsors, fundraisers, volunteers and the general public and ultimately generate a general sense of goodwill in Ireland towards the Games. The company utilised a leading advertising agency in the country (D.D.F.H. & B. Advertising Ltd) to maximise its marketing effort. Their services were supplied free of charge. This was supported by a distinguished public relations company, Fleishman–Hillard Saunders. Decoy provided the design work for the campaign and Media 1 created the website. All of these services were provided to the company free of charge.

MARKETING PLAN

The company created a focused structured marketing plan, which assisted them to achieve their overall objectives of fundraising, increasing public awareness and creating positive attitudes towards the athletes and the Games. A significant feature of the marketing was a determination to keep the focus on the athletes. For example, there was always an athlete in the television advertisements. Training and support for public appearances was provided through the Special Olympics Athlete Leadership Programme. This programme allowed athletes to explore opportunities other than taking part in sports training and competition, and empowered them to take on new and challenging roles as spokespersons, mentors or coaches.

The marketing plan was divided into various projects and objectives. The breakdown of projects was as follows:

Communications
- Look and identity of the Games
- Media services and operations
- Advertising
- Website and publications
- Celebrity plan
- Signage
- Information services
- Sound production
- Documentation

Sponsorship

Merchandise

Each sub-programme developed its own goals and strategies. For example, the goals for the advertising strategy were as follows:

- Create a TV, Radio and Newspaper campaign that builds awareness of Special Olympics and the 2003 Special Olympics World Summer Games
- Establish the theme of 'Share the Feeling' to integrate all activity and communicate a feeling of a 'big event' coming to Ireland
- Create a sense of national excitement and goodwill
- Promote association of sponsors with Games
- Motivate and recruit host towns, volunteers, families to sign up to respective programmes
- Create a campaign to encourage the public to support the Support An

Athlete Campaign and reach the €2.5 million target
- Generate awareness and support for the Torch Run
- Promote the Opening and Closing Ceremonies; recruit attendance at both events and the 22 sport and competition venues
- Communicate thank you message and celebrate achievement.

The outcomes in relation to the adverting strategy were that eleven television, thirteen radio and fourteen print advertisements were produced. In addition to the €1.25 million advertising secured as part of sponsorship agreement with the national broadcaster RTE, approximately €3,032,040 was secured through all other Irish advertising media outlets in television, radio and print. The 'Share the Feeling' theme was established as the Games' slogan. Advertising helped to create a sense of national excitement and goodwill. The association of the sponsors with the Games was successfully promoted through advertising.

Among the key objectives of the advertising campaign was the need to recruit 30,000 volunteers and to create the feeling that the people in Ireland will be participating in a truly unique and special event. All volunteer requirements were achieved ahead of schedule and a waiting list was created prior to the Games to cater for the huge amount of people who had offered their services as volunteers.

The Families Programme (in association with Toyota Ireland) was marketed through television, radio and print. The objectives of this programme were to have 1,000 families in the greater Dublin area open their homes to families travelling to the Games from abroad, to recruit volunteers to assist with the Family Ambassador programme, to increase the awareness of the 2003 World Games and to give an insight into the level of planning and organisation involved. This initiative was so successful that a waiting list had to be established for families wishing to open their homes to travelling participants.

RAISING CAPITAL

The big challenge for most business ventures is raising sufficient capital to enable the business to commence trading. The Special Olympics was no different. In order to stage this world-class event professionally, a large amount of capital had to be raised. This required a resourceful entrepreneurial spirit, extensive planning, creative marketing and public relations. The organisation approached the government, the European

Union, the corporate sector and the general public in its attempt to raise sufficient funding through sponsorship. Sponsorship is defined as investments in causes or events to support corporate objectives, such as an enhancement of corporate image or an increase in brand awareness. In the case of the Special Olympics, this form of sponsorship is known as 'cause-related marketing'. The sponsors did not enter into this arrangement from a sense of altruism, nor were they driven by philanthropic intentions. They believed that their association with this event would assist them in achieving their business objectives.

Although obtaining corporate sponsorship was a financial necessity it was also extremely difficult. The CEO made the initial contact by writing a letter to targeted companies and this was followed by endless phone-calls, meetings and presentations. Following advice from a group of strategy experts from the United States, Davis realised that she was not offering organisations an opportunity to be philanthropic or civic minded. Rather she was selling a hard business proposal that ultimately became enshrined into a legally binding contract. The business community was enticed on the premise of 'cause related marketing'. The notion of buying into a brand, of access to the logo and to the multiple opportunities for promotion and sponsorship were the main features that were attractive to the sponsors.

Particular companies were targeted to become sponsors on the basis that the subsequent partnership could be mutually beneficial. Bank of Ireland became the main corporate sponsor of the event, donating €6 million initially, although Mary Davis suggested that the final figure might have been closer to €10 million. The national branch network of the Bank of Ireland also became a major asset to the organisers, particularly for the Host Towns programme. There were many examples of host town committees being chaired by bank officials and employees of the bank became widely involved in a voluntary capacity. On the other hand, this involvement at a local level gave the bank access to a wide cross-section of the community that they may not have dealt with previously. Five other companies (Eircom, RTE, An Post, Toyota, O'Brien's Sandwiches and Aer Lingus) agreed to provide funding of €1 million each. Eircom installed and provided the IT network free of charge, which represented significant savings for the organisation. Aer Lingus committed to providing free flights on their airline for much of the overseas travel that was necessary. RTE provided the advertising air-time free of charge.

One of the factors that contributed to the success of the sponsorship arrangements, according to Mary Davis, was the fact that the sponsors did not have to compete with each other for publicity. Each sponsor was given a choice of one of the Special Olympics programmes to become associated with, which resulted in dominant branding at each event. For example, Toyota became primarily involved with the Host Family programme as they were trying to sell their cars to the 'family' market. An Post chose to become involved with the Schools Programme as they already had a relationship with schools. In total, over €22 million was raised in corporate sponsorship for the Games.

Attracting sponsorship was not all good news, however. There was a downturn in the IT market in 2000 and an important sponsorship contract that was on the verge of being signed was withdrawn. Much time and effort was subsequently spent on making presentations to companies trying to find a way to provide the necessary 600 computers and associated technology. One of the principal difficulties inherent in any sponsorship activity is trying to evaluate the effectiveness of the investment. Bank of Ireland developed some metrics to measure this. In January 2003, six months prior to the Games, it was the best-known event in Ireland with 98 per cent awareness, and 72 per cent of those surveyed were aware that the bank was a sponsor of the Games. Bank employees also enthusiastically embraced their employer's involvement with 900 volunteering their services and 29 working directly on the Games through a secondment.

PUBLIC FUNDING

The total financial contribution of the Irish government to the Games was €13 million. From the outset the government recognised that winning the Special Olympics Games could have positive spin-offs for Ireland. There would be an international impact due to the worldwide exposure Ireland would have in the lead up to and for the duration of the Games. The organisers hoped to portray the cultural richness of the island, thereby attracting valuable tourism revenue. Mary Davis also suggested that the government was interested in how well the country's infrastructure and facilities could cope with delivering such a large-scale event while being on the world stage. The then Minister for Arts, Sport and Tourism, John O'Donoghue commented that:

> The government has made this commitment because it sees the Games as a unique opportunity to engage the entire Irish community around people with learning difficulties and to do so in a warm and dignified way, which focuses on their true potential and

their true worth. I do not believe that any other initiative could lead to such a profound change in national consciousness and it is the true basis for the widespread social acceptance of people with learning disabilities and the recognition of their true potential.

FUNDRAISING

Fundraising was to become an increasingly important part of the overall strategic planning for the event. A fundraising department was in place by March 2002 and was composed of members of the board, and some patrons and sponsors. It was a strong committee, with a good mix and balance of influential and high profile individuals from many walks of life such as business, sport and entertainment. In addition, there was a good geographical spread in the composition of the committee ensuring representation was countrywide.

The fundraising targets for the committee were established and each committee member was given an area of responsibility and reported progress back to the committee on a monthly basis for the duration of the campaign. The fundraising department grew from two people to the final figure of eight during the twelve months prior to the Games. Staff was recruited on a 'need-to-know' basis. A fundraising ball held in Dublin for the Special Olympics was the single most successful fundraising ball in Ireland to date. An example of the quality of the planning that ensured financial targets were reached or exceeded can be seen in the Support an Athlete Programme. This was the main fundraising project. Initially, at the planning stage it was titled 'Adopt an Athlete' but it was changed in late 2002 to 'Support an Athlete', as this was felt to be a more appropriate title and that it would bring more clarity and focus in the minds of the public.

Table 10.1: **Fundraising Targets against Actual Amounts Achieved**

	Target (€)	Actual (€)
Support an Athlete	2,500,000	2,500,000
Fundraising General	750,000	1,248,243
Golf Events	500,000	530,000
Race Days	250,000	316,000
Balls	250,000	1,406,630
Cash Target	4,250,000	6,000,873
Value in Kind	1,000,000	2,105,295
Total Target	5,250,000	8,106,168

The key deliverables of the fundraising campaign were:

Database of target companies

A database of 2,000 companies countrywide was developed. Each member of the team had responsibility for about 400 companies. Companies were met, or telephoned, sent copies of the newsletter and kept informed during 2002 about the Special Olympics and the World Games.

Promotional campaign

This was targeted at raising the profile and levels of awareness of the Games. It consisted of publishing and circulating newsletters, radio and TV campaigns and follow-up telephone calls from the fundraising managers within the department.

Support an athlete pack

This was a pack sent to companies, schools and sporting organisations giving them guidance on how to organise fundraising events. The pack was prepared well in advance of the campaign and was ready to go six weeks before the campaign started. The day after the launch of the campaign 20,000 packs landed on the desks of the groups that were targeted in 2002. The personalities featured in the pack were RTE Presenters (TV and radio) and were instantly recognised.

Telephone contact

Six people worked on the telephone campaign and their main areas of responsibility were:

- Answering the telephone calls – and the response was incredible
- Following up on their own contacts that they had developed during 2002
- Ensuring that interesting events were highlighted on the radio
- Most importantly looking after all the people who telephoned.

The telephones were serviced from 9a.m. to 9p.m. Monday to Friday from January to mid-April. The telephones were also serviced on Saturdays from March onwards.

Certificates

One of the main selling points of the campaign was that after an individual, school, or company ran their event or sent in a donation (min €1,000) they were then sent a certificate advising them of the name of the athlete they sponsored and details regarding their sport and where they came from. During the Games the sponsors could then follow the progress of their nominated athletes on an especially dedicated website. In addition, if they lived outside Dublin the donor was matched with an athlete from their nearest host town and many of them actually met the athletes they had sponsored. A testament to the success of this particular part of the campaign is that *The Irish Times* sponsored an athlete, received the certificate, tracked the athlete down and featured her on the front cover of the newspaper during the Games.

Monitoring of events

Events were monitored on a daily basis and following the development of an effective database system, information was available on a daily basis on how many events were taking place and where. Event hosts were contacted after their event and encouraged to send their money in. Events delivered money usually within fourteen days. Reminder postcards were issued to people who were delaying.

Thank you letters

In addition to sending a certificate to the donors, they were also sent a thank you letter at a later stage and, where possible, received a visit from a member of the GOC.

THE OPENING CEREMONY

On Midsummer Day in 2003, Croke Park hosted the biggest event in its history; 7,000 athletes, representing 160 countries marched onto the pitch. Two of the most famous and respected men in the world, Nelson Mandela and Muhammad Ali, were on stage to open the event. The Corrs performed the opening set, Riverdance brought 100 dancers on stage, Bono guided Nelson Mandela's entrance, a young athlete carried the Game's flag and the Olympic Flame was lit – just some of the memorable events from the opening ceremony. RTE broadcast the event live on television. Celebrities came out in force to support the Special Olympics athletes from the various countries. Arnold Schwarzenegger and his wife Maria Kennedy Shriver, Heather Locklear, Colin Farrell, Ronan Keating, U2, Pierce Brosnan, The Corrs, Roy Keane and Samantha Mumba were just some of the big names that showed their support with performances, speeches or by just being there. It was no accident that these particular celebrities were present. Keeping the needs of the athletes to the fore, the organisers sought out celebrities that the athletes could identify with, whom they would want to be photographed with and whose autographs they would treasure.

CHALLENGES ALONG THE WAY

The most significant challenge, according to Mary Davis, was the SARS virus, which threatened the participation of a number of athletes in the Games. This affected every organising team because it took up so much time and energy. Davis stated that if the teams had not been so organised prior to this threat, they would not have been able to give it the time and energy that was needed. It affected the planning process as 'people were in the middle of planning ... but they could not plan'. The teams who were planning accommodation, catering and transport were under pressure, as they did not know how many people would be coming. It resulted in tension between teams and strong leadership skills were required to hold the teams together, make decisions and to contain the stress. The team, however, also encountered a number of other significant challenges along the way. Other events (some anticipated, others not) included the changeover from the punt to the euro, September 11th and the decline in the fortunes of Aer Lingus. The potential loss of the sponsorship of Aer Lingus would have been a major blow to the organisers, as they had already made significant commitments to look after the travel arrangements of many of those involved. After some nail-biting time, Aer Lingus made the decision to withdraw from all their sponsorship commitments with the exception of the Special Olympics.

EVERYONE'S A WINNER

The success of the Games cannot be underestimated. As a result of the meticulous planning, organising and 'sheer hard work', Ireland's hosting of the Special Olympics World Summer Games 2003 resulted in a positive outcome for those involved directly with the event or those indirectly influenced by the efforts of the organisation:

- Athletes, coaches, athletes' families and friends, and official delegates were able to enjoy the experience of staying with Irish host families and enjoy the true Irish 'céad míle fáilte' for one week prior to the Games
- The Irish government's sponsorship of €13 million resulted in Ireland successfully staging the biggest international event ever hosted by the state

- The premier sponsor, Bank of Ireland, enjoyed the publicity of being a major sponsor of the event and having that sponsorship acknowledged in the marketplace
- The major sponsorship partners, An Post, Toyota, RTE, O'Brien's Sandwiches and Aer Lingus benefited from dominant branding that maximised their sponsorship investment
- As a result of the extraordinary fund-raising efforts in Ireland by companies, schools and individuals, everyone was involved in the organisation and success of the games
- The Host Town Programme enabled the country to acknowledge that there are people with learning disabilities everywhere throughout our land
- The 30,000 volunteers, who contributed prior to and during the Games have contributed to a legacy. The 'feel-good' factor that encouraged them to take part initially was replaced with positive attitudes and continuous support towards people with learning difficulties.

The athletes' oath, 'Let me win, but if I cannot win, let me be brave in the attempt' now resonates with many people when faced with a challenge and the success of the Games will leave a lasting legacy in Ireland of how careful planning and organising by an entrepreneurial team can benefit everyone.

POST-GAMES LEGACY

When it was over, Special Olympics Ireland set up a Special Olympics Network to build on the work, support, enthusiasm and interest developed by the Games. Bank of Ireland, the main financial sponsor of the Games, dedicated €1 million over two years to assist in the establishment of the Network. The Network aims to set up groups all around the country to support existing Special Olympics clubs and to assist in setting up new ones.

All of the 30,000 volunteers received a letter after the event to ask if they would like to remain involved with Special Olympics. The response was very positive, with 7,000 people replying in the affirmative. Each host town was issued with a commemorative plaque from the Games Organising Committee in recognition of their contribution. Many of the host towns and villages have continued their association with the countries they hosted. For example, Ballygar in Galway, which hosted Afghanistan, subsequently raised €25,000 for the Afghan athletes, all of whom had spent their childhood in orphanages. A piece of sculpture with the name of every volunteer carved into it now exists in the grounds of Dublin Castle, a permanent legacy to the contribution of civil society.

Special Olympics athlete, Catriona Ryan, and An Taoiseach, Bertie Ahern, launched the book *Midsummer Magic*, a pictorial record of the 2003 Games. It is a collection of more than 300 images from the archives of 78 of the press photographers. The pictures chart the memories beginning with the lighting of the Special Olympic Flame of Hope in Athens and finishes with the goodbyes at Dublin airport. *A Feeling Shared* is a DVD and video that was also released to capture the highlights of the Opening Ceremony.

'When the flame went out that wasn't the end' was the view expressed by Julian Davis, press officer for the Games. The legacy did not consist of an Olympic village or a new urban transport link. Rather it left behind a legacy of goodwill and an enhanced understanding of intellectual disability that hopefully will remain for decades. Furthermore, the contribution of the volunteers highlighted the fact that altruism can be enjoyable and beneficial for both donors and receivers. The host town programme involved the whole country in the Games and provided the opportunity for communities to come together and contribute. The injection of social capital and the revitalisation of civic society in Ireland remain enormous.

NOTES
1. This case is intended to be used as the basis for class discussion rather than to illustrate either effective or ineffective handling of a management situation.
2. Pauline Connolly and Geraldine McGing are lecturers in Business Studies at Griffith College, Dublin.

Appendix 10.1

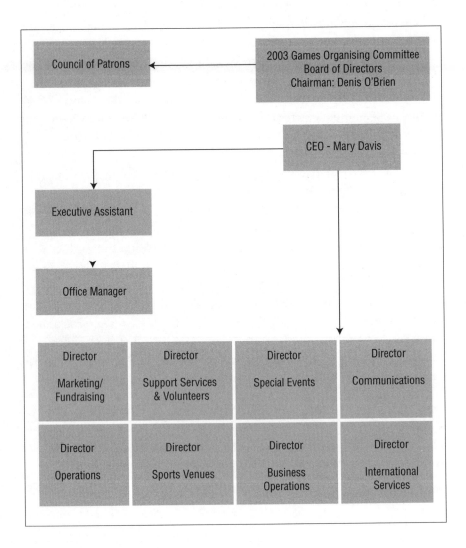

Appendix 10.2

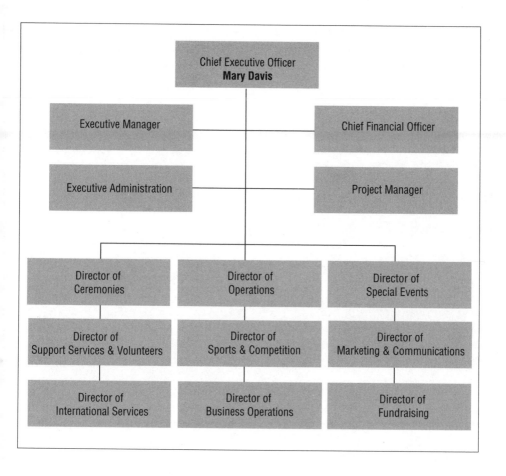